TrumpMania:
Vince McMahon, WWE and the Making of America's 45th President
2020 Election Special Edition

Lavie Margolin

Copyright © 2020 Lavie Margolin

All rights reserved.

ISBN: 9798683844196

A special thanks to the pro wrestling twitter community over the last four years. Your support, knowledge and keen research skills has reignited an interest in something I once loved.

Editor: Justin M Knipper

CONTENTS

	Introduction	1
1	WrestleMania IV	11
2	WrestleMania V	42
3	RAW: Hyping the Battle of the Billionaires	74
4	WresteleMania XXIII: Battle of the Billionaires	129
5	Donald Trump: Owner of Raw	159
6	Hall of Fame	199
7	Donald and Linda go to Washinton	219
	Bibliography	273
	About the Author	299

Who has enough ruthless aggression to reach for the stars as you never have before?
-Vince McMahon, Monday Night Raw, Cleveland, OH, June 24, 2002

I have joined the political arena so that the powerful can no longer beat up on people who cannot defend themselves. Nobody knows the system better than me.
-Donald Trump, RNC, Cleveland, OH July 21, 2016

INTRODUCTION

The 1980s was a time of big personalities, wealth and flashy lifestyles. In an era remembered for Madonna, Michael Jackson and Arnold Schwarzenegger, it would be difficult to say that Donald Trump and Vince McMahon stood out above the pack. But they certainly held their own.

Richard Taskin, a History Professor at North Adams State College wrote that "when the history of the 1980s is written, McMahon will occupy as important a place as Rambo or Ronald Reagan."

Donald and Vince have done and said outrageous things. Their careers have benefitted from others looking the other way. For Trump, it was just "Donald being Donald," and for McMahon it has always been "only pro wrestling" regardless of how many battered bodies and premature deaths of wrestlers in WWE.

Trump captured New York tabloid headlines while growing a real estate empire and McMahon emerged as the Master of Professional Wrestling—even as he professed that he wasn't in competition with other leagues, but was instead fighting for the "family entertainment" dollar against companies like Disney.

As Vince McMahon stated when inducting Donald Trump into WWE Hall of Fame in 2013, the two of them are very much alike. Each had been dubbed the "P.T. Barnum" of their respective fields. One does not have to venture too far to see the connections.

Exhibiting some classic Type A personality traits, McMahon and Trump are very competitive, can get easily wound up, have a heightened sense of urgency and can become angry or hostile. They are also wonderful at promotion. They don't mind inflating attendance numbers that are already good to make an event seem even bigger than it already is, simply because they were involved, whether it is claims of the highest attended inauguration ceremony ever or a WrestleMania event that exceeded 100,000, no matter how many ushers and ticket takers had to be included in the number.

Trump and McMahon, who are similar in age and

height, have deep family roots deep in their primary business interests (real estate and professional wrestling, respectively) that date back to their grandfathers.

While Trump grew up with his father in a wealthy area of Queens, NY called Jamaica Estates and learned the real estate business at his knee, McMahon grew up in a trailer park in North Carolina, and would not meet his father until he was twelve years old. His father, despite or perhaps because of being the son of a promoter himself, told him to find steadier work, like a government job.

While Trump's lineage may seem like a less bumpy ride, it was not without its blemishes. His father, Fred was once arrested for failure to disburse at a Klu Klux Klan rally in 1927 and his grandfather, Freidrich Drumpf (the family's last name was changed at one point), was said to amass his wealth partly by setting up brothels near mining towns. A former colleague at the United States Football League said, "Donald grew up the fourth of five children in a privileged family, and he is still in the race to win enough approval."

McMahon and Trump glowingly wrote about their fathers in the book, *Great Dads: A Celebration of Fatherhood*. Alongside an eclectic collection of celebrity contributions, including George W. Bush, Jesse Ventura, Jay Leno and Christie Todd Whitman, Trump and

McMahon included pieces about their fathers' loyalty and fairness to their employees.

Both Trump and McMahon have involved their children deeply in their businesses and have kept them close by at public appearances, especially Trump's oldest daughter Ivanka, and McMahon's only daughter, Stephanie. Andrea Bernstein, the author of *American Oligarchs: The Kushners, the Trumps, and the Marriage of Money and Power,* describes Ivanka as "an embodiment of a certain view of confident modern womanhood." Stephanie McMahon, current WWE Chief Brand Officer, is the company's public embodiment of work-life balance, and her prowess in life had been planned to be displayed to the world for a now postponed autobiography titled *Lady Balls.* Bernstein also writes of Ivanka that "At crucial moments, she deployed this brand to blunt her father's sharper image." Stephanie, while remaining blunt, has always been ready to defend her father, even at inopportune moments, such as comparing her father's steroid trial ordeal to the attacks on the World Trade Center, a few days after 9/11 on WWE's Smackdown program.

Trump and McMahon have each made the wrong financial decisions at certain points in their careers but have come out on top and are generally seen by the public at-large as flawed but successful people in the world of business. With gambling legalized in Atlantic City in 1976 to help prop up the struggling beach town, Donald Trump began eyeing potential business ventures. He planned on building a casino and hotel next to Convention Hall, now known as Boardwalk Hall. Wary of the Casino Control Commission and challenges in obtaining financing, Trump partnered with Holiday Inns, Inc. to build Harrah's at Trump Plaza, which opened in 1984. It was Atlantic City's tallest building and also had the largest square footage of any casino. A walkway connected the casino to Convention Hall. The casino itself was later renamed Trump Plaza and Trump bought out Harrah's stake for $25 million.

One point of contention, other than the name, was the type of gamblers that the new hotel would seek to attract. Trump wanted to focus on the high-stakes rollers, while Harrah's wanted the middle-market customer as well. When Trump paid $3.2 million to bring boxing super fight Michael Spinks vs. Gerry Cooney to town, big rollers left $7.2 million on his tables. Once Trump was in full control in 1986, however, he realized that he did need the middle market gamblers as well. Bringing WrestleMania to town in 1988 was a strategy to attract that audience and their families.

In 1980, Vince and Linda McMahon founded

Titan Sports. They acquired the Cape Cod Coliseum and not only oversaw Vince McMahon's father's wrestling events taking place at the arena but also hockey games and other touring entertainment. Later, McMahon purchased his father's successful regional wrestling promotion, the World Wrestling Federation. Rather than a one-off payment, the pair agreed to a series of installments, with the deal voided were even a single payment missed. The younger McMahon later described his reliance on future earnings to make these payments as "smoke and mirrors."

Despite being a regionally-based company, the WWF controlled some of the United State's most populous markets, media hubs, and venues for hosting wrestling in places like New York, Boston, Philadelphia and Washington, D.C. McMahon had ambitions of taking the World Wrestling Federation national, a no-no for a business that had for decades been run by regional promoters with respect for a territorial system. By the mid-1980s, McMahon was acquiring the largest stars in the business from rivals to wrestle exclusively for his company, including the crown jewel to help him achieve his ambitions: Hulk Hogan.

McMahon bought television contracts out from under established promoters and had three touring groups crisscrossing the nation almost every night to run shows at locations from the largest arena in the country to high school gyms. McMahon took advantage of his proximity to New York City to leverage media opportunities for exposure, which included relationships developed with MTV and NBC. He understood the potential in a new technology called pay-per-view to maximize his profits, removing the need to rent venues for closed circuit television broadcasts while bringing in more revenue than in-person tickets ever could. The biggest pay-per-view on the WWF's yearly calendar was WrestleMania. It would land in Trump Plaza in Atlantic City in 1988 and again in 1989. Beyond the financial success of the event, a friendship between the McMahons and Trump would begin, which has lasted for more than thirty years since.

"They were both very aggressive in their worlds, masters of the universe in their worlds, very into branding, very *nouveau riche*." Those are the words of Court Bauer, a former WWE producer and wrestling promoter, in describing Donald Trump and Vince McMahon. Donald Trump and Vince McMahon (and Linda) have been friends, business associates and on-screen rivals. The on-screen exchanges were always interesting, if not bordering on obscene.

"He knows I have the grapefruits to give him a patented Mr. McMahon billionaire bitch slap," said

McMahon during one skit. Trump, of course, responded with "Your grapefruits are no match for my Trump Towers." What that meant exactly was not clear, but the audience enjoyed it. What is equally as fascinating is what went on behind the scenes; the intersection of the personal and professional lives of Donald Trump and Vince and Linda McMahon has been quite the winding road since 1988.

What Trump and McMahon may have lacked at times from the general public, and found in each other, is high praise for their respective accolades and positive attention from someone in a similar financial position that each truly respects. The near five-hundred-word Donald Trump biography on WWE.com glowingly demonstrates Trump's contributions to the company.

> "From captivating billionaire to reality TV star, from WWE Hall of Famer to the 45th President of the United States, Donald J. Trump has truly done it all. As one of the most famous men in the world, Trump has been recognized as an innovator of real estate, politics and reality television. And how could you miss him? The Donald's surname—synonymous with wealth and power—has been emblazoned in giant gold letters across skyscrapers and high-rises in the biggest

cities in the world. But long before he stepped into the Oval Office, Trump was helping to shape the future of the squared circle. In fact, he had been making a consistent impact on WWE since the days when Andre the Giant was still king."

Not an appearance went by without McMahon singing the praises of the financial prowess of Trump, even when they were in an on-screen rivalry. Trump has often returned the favor to McMahon, praising McMahon's business acumen and providing the WWF/WWE with mainstream press coverage that only Trump could bring. McMahon, through his own words, or the words of his pro wrestling charges on his wrestling programming, dropped mentions throughout the years that Trump would make for an excellent President of the United States. The bluster and bravado that Trump witnessed at several WrestleManias, whether from a front row seat or inside the ring, surely lent a hand to his memorable electoral debate oratories, his contentious exchanges with the press and his communication with the American public.

What follows is the story, on screen and off, of the mutually beneficial business and personal relationship between Donald Trump, Vince & Linda McMahon and the WWF/WWE. No matter what side of the political aisle you sit on, it would be hard to deny that Vince and Linda McMahon had some hand in the election of the 45th President of the United States, Donald J. Trump.

1 WRESTLEMANIA IV

Atlantic City made filthy rich on the doctrine of never giving a sucker a break, mecca of gullible saps, logical site of WrestleMania.
-The Dayton Daily News

Thank God Donald Trump's a Hulkamaniac.
-Hulk Hogan.

"I really believe that if I'd run for President, I'd win."

Those were the words of Donald Trump in October of 1987 to a reporter for the New York Times in his office in Trump Tower. He disputed reports that he was running for anything and said that he loves what he does. What he did at the time was grow his real estate portfolio that included two casinos in Atlantic City. Daniel Lee, an analyst with Drexel Burnham Lambert, Inc., estimated that after servicing his debt, the casinos afforded Trump about $70 million dollars in cash a year.

James Nold Jr. of *The Courier Journal* wrote on March 25, 1988 that "while half the country is following the presidential-campaign slugfests, the other half is debating the issue of an even more involved and controversial contest: Did Andre the Giant have Hulk Hogan's shoulders pinned? . . . And who will the tournament now set up to fill the now-vacant title?"

As far back as when the organization was known as the World Wide Wrestling Federation, or WWWF, and run by Vince McMahon's father, Vince Sr., the WWF had fairly deep roots in Atlantic City. The promotion was based in the Northeastern United States and toured the region regularly. Nearly any town with a moderate sized population in the area would see the stars come to town several times a year. From 1963 to 1982, there were approximately eighty WWF shows in Atlantic City, an average of four shows per year. This included some years with multiple shows over the summer in the late 1970s, to capitalize on the swelling vacation crowds.

When Vince McMahon Jr. took over the company, the WWF did not return to Atlantic City until 1985, and then stayed away until WrestleMania IV with the exception of The Slammys in 1987. The Slammys was the WWF's over the top, campy answer to the Grammys. The event took place in the Circus Maximus Theater at Caesars Hotel-Casino on December 18 and aired in syndication in 130 markets across the country on December 19. While only one show had been scheduled live, a second was added when tickets for the first sold well.

Outside of the Slammys, if you had happened to be busy in 1985, you would not have been able to have seen the WWF in town for six years. The American Wrestling Association, a Minnesota-based competitor tried to capitalize on the lack of major shows in the market with television tapings at the Tropicana Hotel & Casino in 1985. Unfortunately for the AWA, its top star Hulk Hogan had defected to the WWF several years earlier and their new main draw Sgt. Slaughter, could not drum up the interest in the market that he once had. In fact, the whole roster had been depleted by many defections to the WWF. Only those who were on bad terms with the WWF, too old to be recruited, too young to be ready or were related to company owner and former star Verne Gagne remained.

Trump Casino Hotel hosted a closed circuit broadcast of WrestleMania II in 1986 and was one of several locations that reported capacity or near capacity attendance. An assistant manager at the casino told *The Record*, "We even had a few people leaving the gaming tables to watch these guys . . . it gave people a few laughs."

A WrestleMania II headliner (in a losing challenger to Hogan) and New Jersey native, King Kong Bundy, did come to the city for the Claridge Casino/Hotel grand opening of its second floor wing, connecting the casino to its garage. Bundy carried around a pair of two-foot dice for added attraction.

However, Trump Casino Hotel did not host the closed circuit broadcast of WrestleMania III in Atlantic City. That honor went to West Side Complex.

Linda McMahon testified in the Commonwealth of Pennsylvania before the State Government Ad Hoc Committee of the House of Representatives on June 11, 1987. The McMahons met when Linda was thirteen and Vince sixteen, and they were married in 1966, when Linda turned seventeen. Linda co-founded Titan Sports, the business behind the WWF, in 1980, served unofficially as co-chief executive and finally named President of the company in 1993. She would be named CEO in 2007. As Macho Man Randy Savage put it in 1993, "she is the first lady of the World Wrestling Federation." While joined by Bob Marella (minority owner and long-time performer Gorilla Monsoon) and two members of legal counsel, McMahon presented a pitch to deregulate pro wrestling in Pennsylvania. The efforts were supported by an associate at Kirkpatrick & Lockhart, Rick Santorum. Santorum would be elected later to the House and the Senate and become a leader for the conservative wing of the Republican Party. Santorum spoke years later of his role: "I was at the center of that . . . Pennsylvania was the most pernicious of states when it came to regulation. They made you pay all this money to the boxing commission. They used to just rape these guys." "Rape" is a heavy charge when utilized outside of its intended meaning. Vince McMahon used the term on occasion as an announcer when bringing drama to a storyline unfolding in the ring, such as Andre the Giant getting a forced haircut in the ring: "They are raping him of his dignity!"

Linda openly discussed that pro wrestling was predetermined. It was covered by the Associated Press and in papers like The Morning Call in Allentown, but it caught little national attention. In notable inflation of her own, the commission was left with the impression that the WWF ran about 7,000 events that year (the final number was likely less than a seventh of that). Most interesting was an exchange with a Representative Hughes:

Hughes: "I used to go to the Philadelphia Arena and go to the matches."

McMahon: "Have you stopped going?"

Hughes: "I kind of had to grow up and become a politician."

McMahon: "You're in the biggest arena of them all."

Three years after the first edition at Madison Square Garden, WrestleMania had become the World Wrestling Federation's premier event. It was a lynchpin to McMahon's ambitions: to become the number one wrestling federation around and put the other regional wrestling companies out of business. To this aim, McMahon offered the biggest potential earnings to wrestling stars. The highest profile matches and storylines would occur at WrestleMania. In tandem with the creative hoopla, the event was counted on yearly to be the biggest one-night money maker for the company (and at times, the biggest financial gamble). To increase revenue beyond those that could purchase a ticket in-person, the event was shown via closed circuit location and later via pay-per-view provider, carrying the most expensive price that the company would charge every year for a broadcast viewing. Even today, as a public company, the company (now publicly traded and known as WWE) counts on WrestleMania-related revenue to be a significant contributor to earnings for the year.

The company hosted a tournament on March 27, 1988 to crown a new WWF World Heavyweight champion in Atlantic City, and the one-night tournament was marketed as WrestleMania IV's main draw. The fourth event did not actually take place at Trump Plaza Hotel and Casino but inside the adjacent Boardwalk Hall, which was rebranded for the event. For storyline purposes and to build intrigue, the WWF title had recently been vacated after Andre Roussimoff, better known by his wrestling name, Andre the Giant, defeated Hulk Hogan. In the *Berkshire Eagle*, Hogan was described as "the perfect hero for the salad days of Reaganism . . . . about to crush foreign challengers despite their deviousness." Hogan's entrance theme was a song called "Real American" by performed by Rick Derringer. It begins and ends with the following verse:

> *I am a real American. Fight for the rights of every man. I am a real American. Fight for what's right, fight for your life!*

Upon winning the title, Andre immediately surrendered the belt to wrestler Ted DiBiase, known to fans as the Million Dollar Man. Even within the outlandish storylines of professional wrestling, the world heavyweight championship could not be handed over to another wrestler in exchange for cash. The title was instead put up for grabs in the tournament, to occur in its entirety at WrestleMania IV. The Hogan-Andre match had been the most viewed wrestling program in the history of American professional wrestling, with 33 million viewers and a 15.2

rating on *The Main Event*, an NBC spinoff of *Saturday Night's Main Event*, an occasional replacement for *Saturday Night Live*. WrestleMania IV was hyped and sold around the anticipated rematch between these well-known combatants.

Donald Trump paid a site fee for WrestleMania to be hosted in Atlantic City. This was a novel opportunity for professional wrestling that was more common in boxing, although whole pro wrestling cards had been paid for on occasion by politicians in the south to drum up interest in rallies.

Under regular circumstances, a promoter would pay a venue to host an event and then keep all revenue from ticket sales. When a site pays a promotion to host the event, the venue sells the tickets and keeps the money. The risk was thus removed for the wrestling promoter. The reason behind buying an event such as WrestleMania was the hope that tourists would attend the event and then spend money at the Trump Casino and Hotel.

The late Mark Grossinger Etess, the Executive Vice President of Trump Plaza at the time, stated that, "Donald Trump is making Atlantic City the sports and entertainment capital of the world with super fights like Spinks-Cooney, Tyson-Biggs, Tyson-Holmes and now with WrestleMania IV. This demonstrates Trump Plaza's commitment to host the world's biggest and most popular events."

Boxing found a good partner in casinos. Trump Plaza was the host to six of seven boxing title fights that took place in Atlantic City in 1987. On June 27, 1988 Mike Tyson and Leon Spinks were scheduled to box at Boardwalk Hall (billed, as with WrestleMania IV, as "Trump Plaza") with an expected earnings payout of $30 million. Tyson himself netted $20 million.

The Associated Press reported that Donald Trump did not want to miss out on a money maker and people pleaser like WrestleMania. Trump stated in WWE's documentary *The True Story of WrestleMania*: "I just wanted a piece of it." WrestleMania had drawn a reported 93,000 the year before in the Pontiac Silverdome (although Dave Meltzer of the *Wrestling Observer Newsletter* would later report the actual number as 78,000). "Everybody in the country wanted this event, and we were able to get it," Trump said.

According to Bruce Prichard, a long-time on and off advisor to Vince McMahon (but best known for his on-screen character Brother Love, a takeoff of a 1980s style televangelist, in red face paint and white suit), "Donald had the space, the McMahons understood promotion, and he knew one hand washes the other." According to Vince

McMahon, "Donald Trump is a businessman and he thought that WrestleMania could bring something to Atlantic City that hadn't been there before." The draw of the event for Atlantic City was especially important on what would normally be a sleepy Palm Sunday weekend.

Unfortunately for the WWF and the visual presentation of WrestleMania IV, the audience in Atlantic City was largely composed of gambling regulars who were unfamiliar with the product and thus not into the storylines or into the action. Passionate cheers and boos were hard to come by at the event, hurting the broadcast appeal of the show over pay-per-view and closed circuit television.

The initial seeds for the event were not planted by Trump and McMahon directly. Etess approached WWF executive Basil Devito after the conclusion of a panel discussion on marketing special events to casinos. Etess felt that Trump's casino was not attracting all the different varieties of gamblers in the market. Trump wanted to attract gamblers that would not come just for a Tyson fight: the high rollers were great (and essential to keeping the casino doors open) but he also wanted to find the middle class gamblers, who were in "business for themselves" in South Jersey and Philadelphia. What type of businesses the New Jersey and Pennsylvania gamblers participated in was not specified. B.J. Bethel of the *Sydney Morning Herald* would describe this target market as "ultimately these were the people who would help form the rusted-on Trump political base." It wasn't clear why Etess assumed that this would match the WWF fan base of the day, which was mostly composed of young fans and families rather than the lower-level gambler types who might, or might not, be business entrepreneurs.

The WrestleMania IV program sold at the show was branded with Trump Plaza details, as would be expected. The Plaza was described as glittering and a new standard of excellence. Trump's plans were described as to make Atlantic City the toast of the whole country. The back of the program features the Trump Plaza image and one full page shows Trump Plaza as a corner post of a ring with the description: "The Champions are fighting from a new corner." The big boxing fights were listed along with WrestleMania IV. It was probably not the most engaging read for a fan expecting in-depth insight in the night's matches.

The Trump hype was hardly a one-off. The Tyson-Spinks fight that summer was notable not only for the quick thrashing of Spinks by Tyson and an exclamation point placed on Tyson's status as the baddest man on the planet, but for the over the top hyperbole use by the ring announcer in introducing Trump before the fight began: "He's a man whose success at business epitomizes the American dream, the author of the year's best-selling book *The Art of the Deal*. His vision and accomplishment make him the quintessential entrepreneur. Ladies and gentlemen, New Jersey thanks him—our host for this great evening of championship boxing, Mr. Donald J. Trump." An introduction so over the top that even McMahon's programming would have a hard time rivaling the effusive, and awkward, praise.

A press conference for WrestleMania IV aired in the form of a short NBC special. NBC executive Dick Ebersol had been working closely with Vince McMahon on Saturday Night's Main Event since 1985 and the pair formed a strong relationship; they'd later attempt to supplant the National Football League with the XFL.

Eugene Arthur Okerlund, better known on the air as Gene Okerlund, the WWF announcer and mouthpiece, invited Donald Trump to the stage to kick off the festivities. Trump announced that the event would be big business for Atlantic City and the event would return the following year for WrestleMania V (clearing up any misconceptions that the return date was only confirmed once Trump saw the success of WrestleMania IV). This was the only time that

WrestleMania would be held in the same city two years in a row and the first time that the location of WrestleMania would be announced more than a year in advance. Today an early announcement of the location of WrestleMania has become standard practice to allow fans from all over the world the chance to schedule a vacation and make plans to attend.

Photos from the event show Trump beaming and holding the WWF title in between Hulk Hogan and Andre the Giant. Another photo shows Trump listening intently to Randy Mario Poffo, known as "The Macho Man" Randy Savage, seated at the dais. Apologizing for arriving late to the press conference, Hulk Hogan stated: "I had a helluva reality check just now. As I was coming up here I was stopped by a little boy in a wheelchair who said to me, 'Hulk, you have to win. You are the last American hero.'" Hogan then declared Trump a Hulkamaniac. Trump, described in the *Daily News* as buoyant, said that "this is going to be one of the great events in the nation this year."

Trump was given a title belt to hold for safekeeping prior to the event, because "Donald Trump is the only person in the world who cannot be bought," according to the WWF's on-screen authority figure, Jack Tunney. The belt was put on display at Trump Plaza's

Casino entrance, near the parking lot.

In another press event held at The Grand Hyatt New York, Trump was not in attendance. One member of the press took the opportunity to ask Ted DiBiase if he was as rich as Trump and if he could "buy and sell Donald Trump? Is your wealth that large?" DiBiase responded that it was for him to know and that "Donald Trump doesn't have the character or charisma I have in or out of the ring." Okerlund being humorous, or perhaps cautious, commented directly to Trump's representative on the microphone: "Steve (Hyde) and Mark (Etess), remember he said it when you talk to Donald."

In a writeup in the *Dayton Daily News* ahead of the big event, alongside a caricature sketch of Hogan, Andre and Trump were some statistics under the headline Tough Guys: Hulk (6'8," 330 lbs.) Hogan; Andre the (7' 5," 550 lbs.) Giant; Donald ($$$??,000,000,000,000.00) Trump.

Trump provided a hype video that was played as part of WWF syndicated programming which aired in local markets across the United States in February 1988. In the video, Trump was enthusiastic, calling it an exceptional and exciting event in Trump Plaza. He said that hotels all over the world wanted it, and it was a great honor to have it at Trump Plaza and to be chosen. There was no evidence at the time of a bidding process for the event. According to Trump, more people were looking for more tickets for WrestleMania IV than any event he could remember, a significant claim given Trump's growing reputation for hosting high-profile boxing events.

The WWF thumbprint was all over Atlantic City the week before WrestleMania, including appearances at WWF events by paid celebrity Vanna White of *Wheel of Fortune* fame. Randy Savage and Hulk Hogan's voices could be heard over the speakers on the Trump casino floor, encouraging people not to miss WrestleMania. WWF Chocolate bars were distributed to hotel guests. If one called Trump Plaza and was placed on hold, they'd hear WrestleMania themed jingles and promotions. There were tent cards on the blackjack and Poker tables featuring the WrestleMania logo and pictures of the combatants.

Etess felt that gamblers would spend more if there were a series of events scheduled to entertain wives and children. The Plaza wanted the WWF to arrange and execute the events and Trump paid for it.

There was a "WrestleMania 5K and One-Mile Fun Race," which was sponsored by Trump Plaza Hotel & Casino and the Boardwalk Runners. Bruno Sammartino, "the Living Legend," was the honorary race marshal and starter, with the run beginning on the boardwalk in front of Trump Plaza. Additional events included a Saturday afternoon party, a ballroom party in the evening and a "Bacon, Bagels and Biceps" brunch. The Bushwackers, Luke Williams and Butch Miller—New Zealand natives known for their missing teeth, unkempt look and love of sardines—were in attendance to chow down. The first WWF fan fest was held that weekend. In later years, the fan fest would grow into a full week of programming at WWE Fan Access with the opportunity to meet current and former wrestlers and participate in a number of activities. To capitalize on more families in town, activities of a non-wrestling nature were planned, including a Gloria Estefan and Miami Sound Machine concert at the Convention Center Ballroom. At Trump's other casino in town, Trump Castle, LaToya Jackson would be performing on Sunday as well. WrestleMania started at 4 p.m., while Jackson's concert was scheduled for 7.

Prime Time Wrestling, a WWF program that aired on the USA Network on Monday nights (predating *Monday Night Raw*), was a vehicle to promote WrestleMania and Trump in an episode that aired six days before the show. Hosts Gorilla Monsoon and Bobby "The Brain" Heenan, were on location at Trump Plaza Hotel & Casino. Monsoon served as the straight man. Heenan was more the comedic figure in one of his roles with the company. In his other role, he served as a manager to a rotating cast of troublemakers and villains, who would challenge Hogan in a Quixotan attempt to wrestle the title from him.

"It's all happening at Trump Plaza Hotel & Casino!" The program opened with Monsoon getting out of a limo in front of the hotel and greeting the doorman. Another scene showed Heenan attempting to check-in to the hotel, being told that he did not have a reservation and demanding to speak with Mr. Trump. The Front Desk clerk told Heenan that she did not have a direct line to Trump but could give him a Trump Plaza hat instead. Heenan and Gorilla checked out Gorilla's "room" for the night, The Park Avenue Suite, where Heenan would have to stay in a roll out cot if he could not get a room (in a show of charity by Monsoon), "This is a suite! This is class!" They lunched together with a view of the beach. They played cards, went to the gym and Heenan got a massage.

The show closed with a "Special thanks to Trump Plaza" graphic interspersed among the segments were pre-taped wrestling matches.

Ten million American homes had the availability to order pay-per-view. The show was broadcast in 165 closed-circuit locations and televised in thirty foreign countries. With no NBA games scheduled for the day of WrestleMania, fifteen twenty-three the 23 NBA arenas were booked for closed-circuit broadcast of the event.

The event was a success, but just *how* successful is hard to pin down. Reportedly, 18,000 tickets were sold in advance. The Associated Press reported that "19,000 screaming fans" attended, paying up to $150 per ticket. On March 24, the WWF and Trump Plaza reported that all tickets were sold. The day of the event, the Daily Register listed that "very few" $100 tickets were still available. WrestleMania IV grossed $40,000,000 according to Gannett News Services. According to Dave Meltzer of The Wrestling Observer, the event was very successful but grossed only a little more than half that number, $21,000,000 (in line with the revenue predicted by the New York Times). Ticket sales were reported as $2,000,000 of that total. The event was considered more lucrative than WrestleMania III, held in a much larger venue.

The pay-per-view opened with a slot machine emblazoned with Trump Plaza. The machine spit out coins with one featuring a live shot of the event, a feat of 1980s technical wizardry. The camera cut to the WWF's Gene Okerlund in the ring, "Welcome to the greatest wrestling spectacular of all time . . . here in Atlantic City!"

A prescient qualifier, for sure. Okerlund was an icon of WWF 1980s broadcasts due to a booming voice and a quick wit. His short stature also made for a good visual when standing next to muscled giants.

Gorilla Monsoon and James Janos, known as Jesse "The Body" Ventura, were the event's announcers. Monsoon, inflating the attendance to bring more excitement to the event, said that there were "at least 20,000 or 25,000 in attendance!"

Ventura had retired as a full-time professional wrestler due to health concerns and slid his way into the broadcasting booth but had not yet ventured into the political arena. Trump first met the future Minnesota Governor at the event, a seemingly casual meeting that would be of greater political importance later in both men's careers.

Unlike that night's official main event entrances shown on camera, Donald Trump's entrance to his seat was met with "wild applause," according to the editor of *Art of the Deal*, Peter Osnos. Trump's front row placement would later become notable: he and his then-wife Ivana sat beside his guests for the event, Robert LiButti and his daughter, Edith. Robert could be seen at one point glaring into the camera. Despite this public appearance, Trump stated in interviews in 1991 and 2016 that he had no idea who LiButti was.

LiButti was in fact infamous for his mafia connections and for being strongly tied to John Gotti. LiButti was eventually banned from state casinos. He considered himself a close friend to Trump and also one of his biggest customers.

In 1991, the Casino Control Commission fined Trump Plaza Hotel $650,000 due to the hotel's dealings with LiButti. The hotel accommodated LiButti's demands to keep women and African-Americans away from him. LiButti was also provided by the hotel with luxury automobiles, which he then exchanged for cash. Edith said that her father and Trump travelled together on his helicopter and yacht. One of LiButti's prized race horses was even named D.J. Trump.

Those more famous than infamous at the event included Vanna White ("guest timekeeper"), dressed in a sequined leopard-skin mini dress, and Gladys Knight, who sang the national anthem. Robin Leach, host of *The Lifestyles of the Rich and Famous*, read a hard-to-follow proclamation of the rules of the tournament, with each new sentence uttered beginning with the word "Whereas." Due to Trump's lifestyle, the invitation to Leach was not a coincidence. Leach joined Trump in Atlantic City once again in June of 1990: to celebrate

Trump's 44 birthday and the newly opened Trump Taj Mahal. Leach emerged from the Trump Shuttle, Trump's newly acquired airline. On that date, each implored the crowd not to count Trump out as he had "made a career out of doing what people said couldn't be done."

A battle royal opened the event, featuring stars known as Nikolai Volkoff, a bad guy Russian in the tail end of the cold war, who was actually Croatian, and Sylvester Ritter, a.k.a. the Junk Yard Dog. JYD, an African American man in a dog chain, had the phrase *THUMP* emblazoned on his backside. This was in reference to his ability to deliver a devastating headbutt (unfortunately, an old racial stereotype in the professional wrestling business that African Americans, as well as Samoans, have hard heads). Those watching at home could be forgiven for thinking his tights said *TRUMP*, as viewers were inundated with so many other references to the real estate mogul, and sponsoring venue, during the event.

One undercard wrestler may have made an impression with Trump viewing from the front row: Edward Leslie, the WWF's Brutus "The Barber" Beefcake." Long-time friend of Hulk Hogan and sometimes on-screen "brother," Beefcake's gimmick was centered on wanting to cut someone's hair. Trump may have been impressed with Beefcake's entrepreneurial spirit if he heard a story doing the rounds: Every wrestler was provided with a handful of complimentary tickets, to distribute to friends and family. Beefcake, unaware that Etess was the Executive Vice President of Trump Plaza, asked him to sell the tickets on the boardwalk and come back to him with the money. Etess quickly reported it to Basil Devito, a WWF executive, according to the *History of WrestleMania* book he authored in 2001.

Fans considered the championship tournament to be lackluster. This was partly due to seeing the same wrestlers enter the ring, wrestle a match, and leave the ring up to four times in one night. The main draws on the show, Andre the Giant and Hulk Hogan, whose pictures were featured on an ostentatious piece of furniture in the Trump Plaza lobby, were eliminated early in a double-disqualification, a strategic "out" where neither man would have to lose. Both had been smartly protective of their win-loss records over their careers, at least since the WWF became a national promotion. Andre's pin-fall loss to Hogan at the previous year's WrestleMania was noted as his first "loss" by the promotion which wasn't the case. Before the match, Hogan participated in an intense and impassioned interview with Okerlund backstage. Halfway through the interview Hogan incorporated Trump into his storytelling, following a prediction of slamming Andre into the ocean through the Trump Plaza floor and somehow disrupting the fault lines: "As Andre falls into the ocean floor, and my next two opponents fall into the ocean floor, so will Donald Trump and the Hulkamaniacs. But as Donald Trump holds onto the top of Trump Plaza with his family under his arm, as they sink to the bottom of the sea, thank God Donald Trump is a Hulkamaniac. He will know enough to let go of his material possessions, hang onto his wife and kids, dog paddle to safety and Donald, if something happens to you and you and the Hulkamaniacs run out of gas, hang onto the largest arms in the world and I will backstroke us to safety." Hogan is perhaps the first person to state that Trump has his priorities in order and is ready to put family before wealth. When Hogan's speech concluded, the director cut to Trump signing autographs in his seat, apparently unaware he was a key figure in Hogan's speech and that the floor might collapse below him.

One first round matchup featured Jake "The Snake" Roberts, who brought an actual snake in a bag to the ring, and "Ravishing" Rick Rude., a wrestler memorable for his long hair, Tom Selleck mustache, washboard abs and obscene pelvic thrust. Tongue firmly in cheek, Ventura was concerned for "The Donald": "Donald Trump might be in trouble! His wife might run off with Rude!" Rude was known for mocking opponents by placing a caricature drawing of an opponent's wife or significant other on the front of his trunks. Fortunately, Rude never did feud with Trump or put Ivana on his trunks.

The match ended in a time limit draw and both men were eliminated. Ivana did sit up and notice a competitor in the match, but it wasn't Rude. In a scene not shown on camera and later recounted by Basil Devito in the book *The History of WrestleMania*, Ivana was not seen in the audience after the conclusion of the Roberts-Rude match. When Roberts passed Ivana with the snake in his hands, she had spilled wine on her dress. When security helped her to the back, she asked the guard in all seriousness, why he had not shot the snake. Real estate tycoon, Abe Hischfeld, once stated that he envisioned Ivana as the next Jacqueline Kennedy, a woman of style and grace. Years later, Roberts revealed that the incident was not an accident. He had noticed Ivana not paying attention to the matches, turning herself away from the action, while sipping champagne. Roberts felt disrespected while working to entertain the fans and thought that giving her a good scare would be the best revenge.

Several fans in attendance left before the

tournament final and main event of The Macho Man Randy Savage versus The Million Dollar Man, had concluded. Randy Savage had gained a good deal of attention and momentum since his debut with the federation in 1985. Fans loved to cheer or boo his uncanny intensity and athleticism and could not miss noticing his on-screen valet (and real wife) Elizabeth Hulette, known as Miss Elizabeth. Perhaps some fans didn't need to wait for the match's conclusion because they had seen the issue of *WWF Magazine* was delivered to mail subscribers days prior. The issue referenced Savage having won the tournament, a blunder that was picked up by the wire services. Savage's father, Angelo Poffo, was said to have bet $1 that "the Million Dollar Man" Ted DiBiase would win; a curious gamble for a man who once wrestled as "The Miser."

The Million Dollar Man was known for wearing a jacket to the ring emblazoned with dollar bill signs and for his catchphrase, "Everybody has a price for the Million Dollar Man!" At one point, DiBiase had been considered to win the tournament and the title. Some thought that the Million Dollar Man character was developed to represent McMahon himself.

Bruce Prichard recounted a McMahon story from 1987 that provides the general core of the nature of the

Million Dollar Man character. McMahon was riding first class on an airplane and had selected the non-smoking section as McMahon is notorious for hating smoke. McMahon could smell the smoke coming from a passenger a few seats over and offered the man $100 to quit smoking. The man refused. McMahon kept upping the offers but getting turned down (McMahon would have an on-screen negotiation session with Trump years later that played out similarly). McMahon finally offered to pay for the smoker's seat and $500. Finally the man accepted. McMahon turned to Prichard and said, "See, everybody has a price for the Million Dollar Man." To say that DiBiase portrayed some of the characteristics of Trump as well would not have been a stretch.

After a four hour show that stretched the patience of fans, Randy Savage was crowned WWF champion for the first time. Hulk Hogan helped to turn the tide in Savage's favor by interfering in the match.

Hogan's participation in Savage's post-match celebration with the lovely Miss Elizabeth, clouded Savage's moment of celebration. The early seeds had been planted for a future breakup and a mega main event for next year's return to WrestleMania.

Gerald Morton, an Auburn University Professor, who had a history of studying wrestling had some concerns with the show, telling the Associated Press: "I'm bothered by a lot of the messages we see. There are some dangerous signals that a 10-year-old can't put into perspective: the notion that all foreigners are evil, the equation of violence and sexuality, even the role that women are being cast in." One man that did not leave his seat early was Donald Trump. Pictures in *The History of WrestleMania* book show Trump standing, clapping and beaming when Hogan and Savage shook hands.

An Atlantic City Trump facility would host two professional wrestling cards in between WrestleMania IV and V. Gorgeous Ladies of Wrestling (GLOW) would descend upon the Trump Castle on Sunday, October 30, 1988 at 2 p.m. According to *Central New Jersey Homes News*, the event booking was personally requested by Donald Trump. A Trump public relations executive, Dennis Gorski was described by the Asbury Park Press as learning "what it's like to be a bird" as he was lifted into the air at the press conference by the wrestlers.

A GLOW wrestling card in the ballroom was certainly a lower key affair when compared with a WWF super show. GLOW was in the national consciousness at the time as a highly- rated syndicated program featuring campy women's characters and subtly (or not so subtly) selling sex in the form of women's grappling. Characters on GLOW programming included three versions of "The Farmer's Daughter," Mt. Fiji, Matilda the Hun and Palestina. *The Asbury Park Press* touted the touring troupe's performance above scheduled appearances at the Castle by Aretha Franklin and Lucie Arnaz (daughter of comedienne Lucille Ball).

The Trump Castle sent a postcard to those on their mailing list featuring one image of GLOW wrestler Big Bad Mama, a large woman in painted face and housedress, and another image of a woman in spandex workout clothing getting bitten on the ankle by a fellow grappler. Seemingly, gamblers could get into the event for free by calling to RSVP. It is not clear how many high rollers took Trump Castle up on its offer but the ballroom, a smaller location than GLOW had typically been holding shows in at the time, was packed according to Dawn Maestas, a wrestler known as Godiva. Tickets were $10.

Donald Trump was not in attendance, but his presence was certainly felt. A skit was taped with GLOW star Daisy, most distinguishable for a daisy painted on her face, going on a "date" with Donald Trump. It was called a "Date to Remember." In the skit, wrestlers prepare Daisy for her big evening; a shot of Trump Castle was shown with the girls relaxing on beds in the hotel room. Before

Daisy received word that Trump wanted to take her to dinner, the girls wanted to "sell" her to the hotel as a waitress or maid. The girls didn't want to miss seeing the date for all of the money in the world— "especially Donald Trump's." Daisy finally left in a limo, seemingly to meet up with Trump. Trump's marriage to Ivana wasn't mentioned. Things must have gone well with the girls of GLOW as they'd return to the Trump Castle on March 25, 1989 (just 8 days before the WWF returned with its next WrestleMania iteration). This time, however, tickets were $15.

Perhaps inspired by Trump's success in Atlantic City in the boxing business, Vince McMahon tried his hand at the sport in Las Vegas. The retired Sugar Ray Leonard returned to the fight game against Donny Lalonde in November 1988. Things did not go as well for McMahon in this new business. Just a few days before the fight, 5,000 tickets were still available, and ultimately sold only 5,590 in a 15,000 seat venue. Donald Trump sat with Andre the Giant at the event. Attending the event in Las Vegas left an impression on Trump: "I've always had a good and warm feeling about this town. I really think I'd be good for Las Vegas." Trump said if he did buy something "it would be the most glamorous place in town."

McMahon's father was said to have told him never to get into the boxing business, but the younger McMahon always did things his way. *The Orlando Sentinel* reported that $10 million dollars were bid to secure the fight. Titan Sports claimed a 6.8 percent buy-rate (about 650,000 buys) at the time but upon pressing, claimed it was just a preliminary number. Bob Arum, a kingpin of the boxing promotion game, claimed it was half of the number reported, 3.4 percent. Amazingly, this did not scare McMahon off from never promoting boxing again. Nine years later, a now 40-year-old Leonard returned for another run with ties to McMahon, this time against Hector "Macho" Camacho. Titan Sports was the pay-per-view distributor for the Atlantic City fight. The original distributor (HBO's TVKO) dropped out due to the original promotor, Michael Blutrich of New Contenders, alleged ties to organized crime. Leonard lost, earned $4 million and never fought again. Titan Sports (and later WWE) has never engaged in boxing promotion or distribution again either.

At the 1988 Republican National Convention on August 18, 1988, George H.W. Bush uttered the infamous words, "Read my lips: no new taxes." The phrase was conceptualized by Bush's campaign manager, Lee Atwater. Atwater claimed inspiration for Bush's no new taxes promise from watching Big John Studd complaining about middle class Americans getting ripped off (Atwater kept a picture of Studd clasping him in a headlock behind his desk). One of Atwater's skills was helping his candidate to focus on the negative components of rivals. He was described as using dubious sources to besmirch opponents. *The Miami Herald* described him utilizing this strategy with Roger Stone in 1978 against Charles Ravenel.

2 WRESTLEMANIA V

The whole world is watching.
-*Students* for a democratic society 1960s slogan and WWF 1980s slogan

Linda McMahon participated in a February 1989 New Jersey legislative hearing in an attempt to deregulate professional wrestling in the state. To push deregulation, Linda had to once again commit the ultimate wrestling sin and admit that professional wrestling was fake. Although this may read as somewhat curious today, and things were very much out of the bag at the time, there were still some trappings of secrecy in the business, even in the WWF.

Linda McMahon's participation in the hearings

had two important goals: more revenue and less oversight when deregulation passed. The New Jersey Athletic Control Board had oversight over events taking place at the Trump Plaza, and the potential for big earnings was on the line with WrestleMania coming to town. Without regulation, the board could no longer tax the video replay distribution, pay-per-view and closed circuit revenues. Irv Mushnick, in his book Wrestling Babylon, speculated the savings totaled $600,000. The WWF would also no longer need to ensure that the promoter, wrestlers, referees or even timekeepers held a license in good standing with the state. Perhaps most detrimental to the wrestlers themselves, a physical exam would not be required before the day's matches.

Deregulation in New Jersey did not pass successfully until years later and it led to a public relations headache for the company. Many media outlets picked up on the testimony that was occurring not too far outside of the New York metropolitan market and ran with it. *The New York Times* had a story headlined "Now It Can Be Told: Those Pro Wrestlers are Just Having Fun"

> *"The promoters of professional wrestling have disclosed that their terrifying towers in spandex tights, massive creatures like Bam Bam Bigelow, Hulk Hogan and Andre the Giant, are really no more dangerous to one*

another than Santa Claus, the Easter Bunny and the Tooth Fairy. But please don't repeat this. Millions of grown men and women just don't want to know."

Vince McMahon was surprised at the media reaction and would only allow his wrestlers to appear on programs where he had more control of the script. In an appearance on *Good Morning America*, Vince said that he lied, and that he had only stated that wrestling was fake so the commission would leave him alone. Rival wrestling promoters around the country, who had been greatly hurt by the WWF's aggressive expansion, tried to capitalize on the WWF's admission by saying their promotions were the real ones. Jesse Ventura would mirror McMahon's sentiments in an interview with Roy Firestone, stating that the WWF would say anything to get the commissions off their backs. Ventura challenged anyone who doubted the legitimacy of professional wrestling to face him in the ring despite his being retired.

Trump Plaza Hotel and Casino would once again host WrestleMania in 1989, with Hulk Hogan set to challenge for the championship of "Macho Man" Randy Savage one year after Savage won it. The match was highly anticipated as it was a rare wrestling grudge match that had been built with precision for a full year. Seeds of jealousy over the WWF title and the lovely Miss Elizabeth had been sown. The fans were not used to seeing Hogan without the WWF title for such a long stretch following his emergence as the most popular star of the company in 1984.

The final build to the main event occurred on a live NBC special, the aptly-titled *The Main Event*, again the key catalyst in advancing storylines to peak at WrestleMania. Hogan and Savage, had formed an unlikely regular tag team alliance dubbed the Mega Powers. While at ringside for a Mega Powers match, Elizabeth was injured and Hogan left the match abruptly to check on her. Savage was left to fend for himself against the Twin Towers of Ray Traylor, known as The Big Boss Man, a stereotypical police officer from "down south," and George Gray, known as Akeem, "the African Dream," a massive white man appropriating a hodgepodge of African culture. After a terrible beating, Savage finally made his way to the back and saw Hogan standing over Elizabeth. Savage was filled with rage and told Hogan that he could see his "jealous eyes." Things built to a dramatic peak when Savage hit Hogan over the head with the WWF title belt. The match for the title was on.

Trump was impressed with the success of the previous year and signed up again, as stated in *The True Story of WrestleMania*: "I never sold tickets to anything so easily as I have to this." Two thousand additional tickets were added to the convention center to accommodate fan demand. *Florida Today* expected 21,000 fans in attendance at the Trump Plaza Hotel and Casino. The old Boardwalk Hall took on a grander look for this event.

According to WWE's Hall of Fame announcement video for Trump, "WrestleMania [IV] created such an economic boom for Atlantic City, that Donald Trump fell down and brought WrestleMania [V] back to Trump Plaza."

The WWF must have been looking forward to a return as, according to Basil DeVito, "no one had ever treated us better than the people at Trump Plaza." After attending the event, fan Emilio Delia, said, "It's real only to Donald Trump: real money."

Long-time WWF employee and former ring announcer Howard "The Fink" Finkel described Atlantic City as a thriving place at the time, including options for older and younger people to be entertained. Atlantic City had "vigor, it had vitality and it also had Donald Trump. Donald Trump is one of the most successful entrepreneurs in history." Finkel said Trump's expertise and the WWF's knowledge was a winning combination. It's worth noting Finkel was known for his unyielding loyalty to the WWF as well as his optimism; he was even credited with developing the name WrestleMania.

In promoting WrestleMania V, Donald Trump's name was invoked to build credibility by Steve Planamenta, the WWF's media coordinator: "It's entertainment and we won't make no bones about it. Hey, Donald Trump wouldn't get involved if it wasn't a success. This is our Super Bowl."

Prime Time Wrestling would host another countdown to WrestleMania on the USA Network. Hosts Monsoon and Heenan would once again be on location from Trump Plaza Hotel and Casino. The show opened with Heenan looking for Gorilla in the lobby. Gorilla reminded us that "tickets here are history!" There was a helicopter shot of the hotel from above. The words TRUMP lit up the night in red. Much of the program was filmed from the casino floor. Local gamblers looked indifferent to the wrestling personalities that had invaded their gambling den.

The cable pay-per-view universe had expanded to twelve million potential customers, with one million pay-per view buys expected for the show. The actual pay-per-view figure was 767,000 purchases, still a hit and apparently beating out the Tyson-Spinks championship boxing match. The event was expected to be available in 135 closed circuit locations but was only shown in 64 locations. One edition of USA Today highlighted the conflicting numbers: A story about WrestleMania listed that it would be shown in the 135 locations but an advertisement in the same paper listed only the 64 spots. At the time, it was the highest grossing pay-per-view event. The event featured appearances by celebrities Morton Downey Jr. and rappers Run DMC. The event program magazine listed the Trump Plaza as an undisputed champion, after hosting fifteen world boxing championships along with WrestleMania IV and V.

The show opened with a graphic of the main event, the clash of the Mega Powers, Hulk Hogan versus Randy Savage. In a bit of a surprise, there was no casino or Trump signage included in the graphic. Ted DiBiase, now with a "Million Dollar Belt" in his possession, participated in a backstage interview. DiBiase said that the people that are in attendance were his type of people, people from his sort of club, the elites, like Donald Trump. Later in the show, DiBiase showed Trump his belt at ringside. Trump took a good look as Jesse Ventura commented, "That belt opened Donald's eyes, didn't it?"

Interspersed through the show, viewers received brief glimpses into some of the events that took place over the weekend. Similar to last year, the Bushwackers were enjoying the Bagels, Bacon and Biceps brunch. Harry

Fujiwara, known as Mr. Fuji, playing a stereotypical portrayal of a Japanese man (actually an American, born in Hawaii) as sneaky, participated in the 5K race by jumping the gun and getting off to an illegal head start. Jake Roberts returned to the event with his snake. All was forgiven for last year's incident, or perhaps Trump even got a kick out of Ivana's reptilian scare. "Ravishing" Rick Rude, in a nod to the event's location, called the crowd "high-rolling, Atlantic City sweat hogs."

Trump was interviewed at ringside by Sean Mooney. Mooney referred to Trump as "illustrious" and had trouble pronouncing Trump's name. Trump, with typical bravado, said the event had brought fans from thousands of miles away, it had been unbelievable, fantastic and he was honored. Trump went on to say that it was a big boon to the town, that the casinos (or, at least those bearing the Trump name) were packed. Mooney concluded that, "While Hogan and Savage still have to worry about winning, it appears Donald J. Trump already has."

Trump's interview was a lull in an otherwise good show according to Tom Shales, a TV critic whose syndicated column appeared in many local newspapers. Mooney appeared uncharacteristically nervous while interviewing Trump, as he never seemed rattled before while interviewing world champions and 300-pound combatants. Mooney described the interview as his worst with a celebrity and he was chided by McMahon backstage. Sitting a few rows behind Trump and Ivana was his then-mistress, Marla Maples, a fact that was not brought to light until years later when it was covered on the *Lapsed Fan* podcast.

Hulk Hogan gave a final backstage interview before his anticipated main event. The Trump name was invoked once again by Hogan in a particularly intense and rapid fire interview. Hogan discussed his surprise at facing Savage, in Trump Plaza, one year after Savage's historic win at the previous year's WrestleMania. In anticipation of his match against the Macho Man, Hogan was once again concerned about the foundation of the building: "But just like Donald Trump, Macho Man, I hope you are ready, brother, because Donald Trump has questions in his own mind. He sent a whole team of seismologists [*sic*] out here to check the foundation of the Trump Towers [Hogan could be forgiven for confusing one of the many Trump properties with another] because when the Mega Powers explode on the launching pad, as we erupt over the whole Atlantic City, [Trump] was worried about the foundation, he was worried that the thousands of people in the arena might become unseated and be swallowed by the earth."

Hogan did his best to reassure Trump as he continued: "Donald Trump, don't worry about my Hulkamaniacs. They are survivors. They are ready."

Thankfully, Hogan's predictions of a crumbling building would go unfounded for a second year in a row. There was no indication that Trump was overly concerned about disaster striking (unless perhaps Ivana and Marla met on the way to the restroom). The biggest threat to the fans becoming unglued from their seats would be if the gamblers met the event with the same apathy as the previous year and the event ran as long as last year's tournament.

The Mega Powers were finally ready to clash. Both men were accompanied to the ring by security guards with t-shirts emblazoned with Trump Plaza lettering. During the main event, a particularly heated exchange between Randy Savage and Miss Elizabeth got Donald Trump to jump up from his seat for a better look at the action. In the ending sequence, Savage hit his patented flying elbow drop, a leap from the top rope onto his opponent, with the point of Savage's elbow leading the way. He attempted a pinfall but was pushed off by Hogan. Hogan "hulked up" (pumped himself up via various body gyrations), connected with a big boot on Savage and pinned him for a three count and the win. Hulk Hogan regained his championship and prevailed in another battle of good versus evil. Hogan's song "Real American" played in the background. Announcer Gorilla Monsoon could be heard before the broadcast goes off the air: "Once again, history has been made in Atlantic City!" The *Asbury Park Press* described it as good triumphing over evil.

Later that year, The Rolling Stones came to town for the *Steel Wheels* tour. Ron Ardente, a T-shirt vendor, described sales at the concert as "not bad, not bad." Ardente went to say that "tonight, this has been the closest to what we get for WrestleMania." Hogan and company were the real rock stars by the shore that year.

Bruce Prichard lent insight into the WWF's impression of dealing with Trump for WrestleMania IV and V: "Donald Trump was a joy to deal with, a true professional. He did everything first class. A great partner. A great partner to do business with."

The WWF never did return to the Trump Plaza Hotel and Casino for a wrestling show. The fans at the Atlantic City event were fairly disengaged and which left the show feeling lackluster. McMahon may have been ready to move on. One WWF employee left the company a few months after WrestleMania V to join Trump Sports and Entertainment. Michael Weber, the WWF's Director of Media relations since 1986 joined Trump's organization as Marketing Manager for about a year (Weber is still in the sports and fight game today, serving as the COO of the FITE app). One of those reasons the WWF did not return under Trump's banner may be that Etess, a key Trump staffer and coordinator in overseeing the Trump side of the WrestleMania events, died tragically in October 1989. The helicopter he was travelling in crashed as he returned from promoting another Trump Plaza championship boxing event (Hector Camacho vs. Vinny Pazienza) at a press conference in Manhattan.

Although seemingly WWF fans had enough of WrestleMania in a casino atmosphere, the fact the WWF's biggest show would not return for a third year was of some disappointment in Atlantic City. In January 1990, the Courier Post featured an article titled "A.C.'s Wrestling won't Materialize." Gary Selesner, a Trump Plaza Executive Vice President, explained that "They (WWF) like to set new precedents every year." The seaside gambling town had become old hat. However, when Trump Plaza was scheduled to close in 2014 after limping along for several years, Keith Ingrund, a Pittsburgh native who'd been traveling to the town for many years, remembered the big moments: "I remember how lively it was- with concerts, fights, WrestleMania."

Donald Trump would skip WrestleMania VI in

Toronto, the first time the event would appear live outside of the United States. The event featured another rare loss for Hogan in an attempt to "pass the torch" to the company's hottest rising star, the Ultimate Warrior. One of the event's oddest segments was the Bolsheviks singing the Russian national anthem in the restroom as part of comic relief during the event. One of the event's celebrities, Steve Allen, played the piano while pseudo-Russians Nikolai Volkoff and Boris Zhukov sang along. At least Volkoff, of Croatian origin, was born in Europe. Zhukov, on the other hand, who bore a Russian sickle on his wrestling tights, was actually born in Roanoke, Virginia as James Harrell. Early in his career, he played the patriotic protégé of Sgt. Slaughter as Private Jim Nelson.

But poking fun at the Russian Bear was getting stale, even in 1990. The Cold war was limping to its official conclusion by that point. Trump was not completely out of the news when it came to the event. *Detroit Free Press Wrestling* writer, Bobo "The Half" Nelson wrote that he'd prefer to have seen Donald and Marla Maples versus Ivana and Liz Smith instead of the scheduled intergender tag team match. Smith, a New York gossip columnist, had reported the couple had a mutual love for watching television and eating cheeseburgers.

Jesse Ventura served as mayor of Brooklyn Park,

Minnesota from January 11, 1991 to January 13, 1995. Brooklyn Park hero had a population of 55,000, making it the sixth most populous city in Minnesota. When he suggested council members to "fight it out" and pretended to hit a city council member on the head, it wasn't taken well, regardless of his pro wrestling past.

Ventura became involved in politics when a marshland had been designated for real estate development near his Minnesota home and he was opposed. The developer demanded that his neighborhood install storm sewers, gutters and curbs, which would lead to an increase in cost for homeowners and a runoff into the wetland, which could have destroyed it. His campaign included expanded recycling programs, two-term limits for city officials and slow growth development. In a contentious city council meeting, Ventura said, "You're going to make me run, aren't you?" Mayor James Krautkramer and his followers thought he had no chance of winning, in Ventura's assessment of the situation.

Ventura ran successfully for Mayor on the slogan, "If you've had enough and you're mad enough." There were no debates and the Associated Press described it in 1990 as a contest "mostly waged by yard signs." Ventura's signs kept disappearing. He would sit by the signs on weekends to make sure that they did not disappear.

Ventura said he did not spend more than two or three thousand dollars on the campaign. He and his supporters followed a grass roots strategy of knocking on doors. His campaign volunteer numbers grew to such a degree that Ventura for Mayor literature was dropped off at every home in the area in one day, Ventura claimed. Krautkramer, who had served in office for eighteen years, acknowledged Ventura was a threat: "He's been doing this for a year and a half and I don't have the ability to come up with the one-liners that he does." Ventura won in all twenty-one of the city's precincts with a total vote of 12,728 to 7,390. Needless to Say, **VENTURA** looks better on a sign than **KRAUTKRAMER**. Ventura was in a jubilant mood, "We broke open the champagne about midnight and we were up until about 4 a.m." The job was part-time and paid $900 a month.

Ventura planned for the mayoral job to be the beginning and the end of his political career but he left the window open, "I'd like to say this is the end but four years from now I might be Senator Ventura." By 1994, Ventura did live up to his word of not running for mayoral re-election: "I rode into town, I ran the bad guys out of town, and now it's time for me to ride into the sunset with a hearty 'Hi-ho, Silver'"

In speaking about his overall political

qualifications, Ventura said, "Aren't we all qualified to serve? I believe that's what our forefathers had in mind—that all butchers, bakers, candlestick makers and former pro wrestlers can all serve." Ventura has described how pro wrestling had prepared him: "My most important legacy was learning how to perform . . . I can do the job. It's not like transplanting kidneys . . . I've got to say, I don't find a lot of elected officials to be all that bright."

Trump was in attendance for WrestleMania VII in Los Angeles. Originally scheduled for the 100,000 seat Coliseum, the WWF publicly announced that they had moved the event to the smaller Los Angeles Memorial Sports Arena due to security concerns. "Iraqi sympathizer" Sgt. Slaughter was in the main event and the company claimed that he was receiving bomb threats. It was a difficult road for Slaughter to take to make his way back to the company. Although foreign war rivals had been an easy storyline to exploit within the context of pro wrestling,, characters were usually used after wars had ended, like when there was an influx of faux-Nazi characters popping up in the 1950s, for example.

Ironically, Slaughter had been a flag waving patriotic hero to fans of the WWF over the course of his last appearance in the company. His deep voice and passionate yelling of the Pledge of Allegiance was a particularly engaging crowd pleaser. Slaughter never actually served in the Marines, despite claiming that he had in a variety of interviews. He had left the company in 1985 on bad terms, said to be over a GI Joe toy licensing deal or a request for extended vacation time.

Controversy over the storyline led Bob Costas, a long-time pro wrestling fan from St. Louis, a traditional pro wrestling stronghold from before the WWF's aggressive expansion, and a well-respected NBC sports broadcaster, to cancel his appearance in the event. Costas and McMahon would meet in a contentious interview years later on HBO's *On the Record* program.

The truth was that ticket sales, while selling at a steady pace for an arena event, would have made for a cavernous open space of empty seats if held inside a massive stadium. Only 14,000 seats had been sold for a 100,000 seat Coliseum. The event was deemed an instant sellout when it was moved.

To build up the show, a WWF special aired on NBC, *The Main Event V*, with Hulk Hogan visiting the troops on a military base, which aired in February 1991. The ratings were a disaster—a 6.7, the lowest number to date—, and it ultimately led to them cancelling WWF *Saturday Night's Main Event* program. The WWF's time as a hot promotion was sputtering to an end, and the product would be ice cold within a few years.

Trump was front and center for the most patriotic of WrestleManias. The announcers deemed it as the "Stars & Stripes" edition. The arena was draped in red, white and blue, and fans burst into chants of "U-S-A! U-S-A!". Hacksaw Jim Duggan was dressed as Uncle Sam. Trump wasn't just there for fun, though. His girlfriend at the time, Marla Maples, was part of a celebrity co-host triumvirate that also included Regis Philbin (whose fandom was obvious, given the steady flow of wrestlers as guests on his morning show) and *Jeopardy!* host Alex Trebek.

Maples was more infamous than famous at the time. She became a regular of the New York tabloid scene. In headlines that would rival the Hogan- Miss Elizabeth- Savage love triangle, Trump and Maples would become regular cover stories for the New York Post. Stories from 1990 included "SPLIT: Trouble in paradise as Donald Trump walks out on Ivana"; "The Trump affair: DON JUAN! Secret visits to model Marla at Hotel St. Moritz hideaway"; "Donald and Marla used to share the same pew ... THEY MET IN CHURCH"; "Marla boasts to her pals ... BEST SEX I'VE EVER HAD!" and on and on. Trump and Ivana would divorce in 1992.

Maples had two specific roles as a guest celebrity, described by announcer Gorilla Monsoon as the "unenviable task of locker room reporter and main event bell keeper." Okerlund interviewed Maples backstage. Maples said she was "gonna call 'em the ways she sees 'em." Okerlund quipped in response that "there will be a lot of cold showers tonight." Maples rang the bell for the main event in a white sequined mini-dress. She also conducted backstage interviews with heels (bad guys) The Nasty Boys, Jerry Sags and Brian Knobs, as well as their on-screen manager, Jimmy Hart. The interview with Hart and the Nasty Boys occurred after their tag team title win over the Hart Foundation. One of the Nastys gave Marla a kiss on the cheek . There was a lot of screaming and champagne flowing. Bobby Heenan quipped "She'll have to change dresses if we are going out tonight"

Jake "The Snake" Roberts claimed he had a chance to speak with Maples at the event. According to Roberts, Maples told him that he was Trump's favorite wrestler (due to Roberts scaring Trump's wife, Ivana, with his snake at a previous WrestleMania). Maples' participation was mocked by syndicated newspaper columnists O'Malley and Collin, who sarcastically said that her career really must be looking up and noted that she used to be more selective about projects.

In 1993, Trump would marry Marla a couple of

months after she gave birth to a daughter, Tiffany. Tiffany was most notable during Trump's presidential election bid as being the least visible of Trump's five children from three women. Trump and Maples would divorce in 1999.

As was visible to viewers at home, Trump and his guests often left their seats for several matches during WrestleMania VII, an occurrence that could not have pleased McMahon, for whom appearance was everything. The WWF has even hired people as seat-fillers at big events to ensure the right look on television, but this wasn't something you could do with Trump's seat in the front row. Most notably, Trump missed the WrestleMania debut of a one Mark Calaway, known to most as the Undertaker.

One of the wrestlers said to be spending the most time around Trump was "Million Dollar Man" Ted DiBiase. DiBiase's on-screen character was well known for shoving hundred dollar bills down his prone opponents' throats. In an out-of-date storyline, DiBiase was feuding with his African-American former "man servant," Michael Jones, known as Virgil. Virgil said that the word "'man" was spelled V-I-R-G-I-L.

Trump returned to his seat later in the show and was once again front and center to see America (in the form of Hulk Hogan) triumph over an Evil Foreigner. The

WWF faced sharp criticism for the use of the Gulf War to further storylines. Slaughter went so far as to burn a Hulk Hogan t-shirt as a stand-in for the American flag. Despite needing the job, Slaughter could only take things so far. Thankfully for the WWF and its public image, the war had ended prior to the event taking place.

Not to miss out on another opportunity to interview Trump, Okerlund spent a few minutes on camera with him. After being introduced as "the man who engineered *The Art of the Deal*," Trump called the event unbelievable and said it was a fantastic job. He loved it and had brought a group of people with him. Okerlund said that he hoped the WWF would be back in Atlantic City for WrestleMania very soon to which Trump responded, "We hope very soon."

WrestleMania never returned to Atlantic City or any Trump branded venue. The previous year, Trump was $900 million in debt and faced bankruptcy. Trump's foray into boxing began to unravel when his biggest drawing card, Mike Tyson, lost unexpectedly to Buster Douglas in Japan on February 11, 1990. Trump had been an advisor to Tyson for eighteen months leading up to the fight. Some would say that was a conflict of interest as Trump would often do business with Tyson, hosting his fights under his casino's umbrella.

Evander Holyfield versus George Foreman on April 19, 1991 was the last major boxing match promoted under Trump's watch. Trump overbid to secure the fight, to a tune of $11 million. McMahon's WrestleMania VII may have been negatively affected by Operation Desert Storm, but to Trump, it was an opportunity to save money. Trump utilized an "Act of War" clause in the contract to negotiate for around half of the agreed upon amount with promoters Main Events and Top Rank. Trump was sly in leveraging the opportunity against the promoters as it would have been more costly for them to fight the issue in court, move the date and possibly start promotion all over again in a new venue and town.

Titan Sports, parent company of the WWF, did return to a Trump-owned Atlantic City venue a few years later for the World Bodybuilding Federation Championships in June of 1991. It was the first McMahon produced event to take place at the Trump Taj Mahal. 4,200 fans attended, but only 2,300 of those tickets were sold.

To announce the formation of the WBF and hype the venture, McMahon held a press conference on January 30 at the Plaza Hotel in New York City. Trump had purchased the Plaza Hotel on March 28, 1988—just one day after WrestleMania IV—for $407.5 million. A

Manhattan landmark, it had been on Trump's radar since he was in his twenties. At one time The Plaza had billed itself as "the world's most luxurious hotel." It had eight-hundred rooms in a French Renaissance style and had been the home of luminaries like F. Scott Fitzgerald and Frank Lloyd Wright. Trump said that he could see the building out his window and had to have it. He considered it the equivalent to purchasing the Mona Lisa. Trump negotiated with the previous owner to avoid a bidding process and acquire the property through negotiation. Ivana was named as the Plaza Hotel President. Her salary was said to be $1 plus all the dresses she would desire. The Trumps went into renovating the grand hotel in a way that wouldn't be too expensive. Trump made sure all the ashtrays were stamped with the Trump logo. The Plaza Hotel would go into bankruptcy in November of 1992.

The thirteen stars of the WBF, ten of whom were defecting from bodybuilding industry leader Joe Weider's IFBB, were announced at the press conference. Each was wearing black tank tops, tight shorts and neon green jackets. They were referred to as WBF BodyStars (in a similar marketing attempt to referring to wrestlers as Superstars). Each BodyStar gave a brief speech. In a bit of a stretch, Tom Platz, the WBF's Director of Talent Development, said that one day Magic Johnson would come up to a BodyStar and tell him that he'd watched the BodyStar on television the night before. To promote the event, BodyStars would face WWF Superstars in competition on *Family Feud*. Special workout segments appeared on the WWF's syndicated programming.

Nelson Sweglar, the WWF President of Television at the time, watched the rehearsals in the Trump Taj Mahal and knew that it would not be a successful event. Gary Strydom won the competition, with Mike Christian coming in second. Strydom was rumored to be earning $400,000 per year in a three year deal at a time IFBB participants were earning up to $50,000 per year. Strydom was portrayed as the "Toast of the Town," with top hat and cane. Each bodybuilder was given a character, such as "Bat Man," "Iron Warrior," "Dark Angel" and Tony Zuccolotto as a California beach surfer, board and all.

Donald Trump sat in the front row, along with Marla Maples (who had moved up in stature and seating row since WrestleMania V) and Regis Philbin. McMahon co-hosted the event with Bobby Heenan.

Heenan was known for his quick wit and sharp sense of humor but not even Heenan, along with Vince McMahon himself, and a small assist from Trump, could make an event like this exciting. Each bodybuilder was given a two-minute introductory video. In one segment, BodyStar Barry Demey was shown in Trump Casino wearing a tux, surrounded by gorgeous women, and playing roulette. The skit continued with one of the women inviting Demey back to her room where they undressed (under the sheets and not visible to viewers) and sipped champagne. Demey interrupted the steamy moment as he had to leave to go onstage to the competition. When he was done posing, a video showed Demey going back to the room.

A curious fact came out later: the BodyStar with the highest contract was also the first place winner, the second highest paid BodyStar won second place and so on. The fix may have been in. So few videotapes were sold of the show when it was commercially released that it is considered a collector's item. Due to steroid scandals and no signs of a financial return, the federation was discontinued by July 1992 after a second pay-per-view was said to have sold only 3,000 buys. Titan Sports was reported to have lost $15,000,000 on the endeavor. McMahon called Joe Weider to concede defeat.

Just one month following the WBF pay-per-view event, Vince McMahon was facing allegations of steroid distribution. To publicly combat these allegations, Titan Sports held a press conference at the Plaza Hotel on July

16 1991, where he had paraded his newest World Bodybuilding Federation muscle men just half a year earlier. Vince McMahon revealed that he had experimented with Decadurabolin, which he purchased from Dr. George Zahorian over a four-year period. McMahon said that he was no longer using steroids himself and that he would be willing to be steroid tested. McMahon noted that a new drug testing policy would be implemented by Titan Sports to ensure clean athletes.

A rival to the WWF scheduled an event on February 29, 1992 at a Trump owned facility but it did not happen as planned. World Championship Wrestling, a Ted Turner property whose programs aired on TBS, scheduled the second edition of one of their annual pay-per-view shows, SuperBrawl, at the Trump Taj Mahal in Atlantic City. WCW had rolled into town the previous year, on March 3, 1991 for an un-televised house show. The company was undeterred from returning for a pay-per-view despite only drawing 1,800 at the event, slightly above the average attendance in a bad business year for the struggling organization. The SuperBrawl II main event was scheduled to be WCW star Sting, against Lex Luger. The event had to be moved to Milwaukee because of a new pay-per-view idea by Trump: One-on-one basketball between two legendary players as "Dr. J" Julius Erving agreed to play Kareem

Abdul Jabbar. The basketball game required an extra day's setup, disrupting the ability to host the wrestling show. The game was panned by critics and basketball purists.

The WWF continued to invoke Trump's name to build credibility by association for the company. Sid Eudy, known as Sid Justice, an up and coming star placed as the heir apparent to Hulk Hogan, mentioned Trump in promoting an upcoming WWF television taping in Nashville, Tennessee's Municipal Auditorium. A 1992 article explaining how the audience has changed that was run in the *Tennessean Showcase* quoted him saying "Our audiences are now more intelligent. It's no longer a redneck who comes in overalls, but people like Donald Trump come to our matches."

In 1993, Connecticut Governor, Lowell Weicker, Jr., named Vince and Linda McMahon to the 1995 Special Olympics Board of Directors. Weicker and the McMahon's were described as neighbors in a 1994 Hartford Courant Article.

WWF would return to Atlantic City on June 30, 1993, without the involvement of Trump. When the WWF did finally return for a non-televised house show in the ballroom of the convention center, the wrestling business had grown colder due to scandals, lack of new stars and uninspired storylines. There were some familiar faces on the underwhelming six-match card: Ted DiBiase (as part of a tag team main event), former bodyguard Virgil (in a singles match win to open the show), and Randy Savage, winding down his WWF in-ring career. The stars were not all in attendance as the WWF ran three shows, in three different cities, on the same day. The WWF would take a rare few days off and would reconvene to hold a patriotic celebration on the deck of the USS Intrepid in honor of the Fourth of July with the main attraction being to learn who could slam a gigantic evil Japanese foreigner named Yokozuna (who was, in fact, Samoan). US dignity would be restored by a reformed Lex Luger, who would slam the evil foreigner, and would soon enough be draped in red, white and blue.

The US Attorney's office of the Eastern District of New York charged McMahon in 1993 with possessing illegal steroids with the intention to distribute them to his wrestlers. The evidence included a memo from Linda McMahon to Pat Patterson. Patterson, born Pierre Clemont, was a former wrestler and long- time trusted confidant of the McMahons. In the confidential office memo from December 1, 1989, released to the public but with redacted portions, Linda McMahon suggested that now was a good time to cut ties with Zahorian and to alert him that the Justice Department was considering action.

There was a reference to previously considering having Zahorian return to events, as Patterson is alleged to have said that the boys need their "candy" (steroids). At the time of his arrest, Zahorian was said to be shredding related paperwork in his office. This memo was considered a "smoking gun."

During the 1994 trial, Afa of the Wild Samoans sat staring at the jury, mouthing the words "Not Guilty." Hulk Hogan was expected to be the prosecution's star witness. To the government's surprise, he said that McMahon had never tried to sell him, or ask him to take, steroids. The case against Vince McMahon's alleged steroid distribution fell apart due to procedural errors on behalf of the district attorney. McMahon was acquitted of one charge by the jury while the judge dismissed the remaining two charges. Afa the Wild Samoan was certainly pleased.

At WrestleMania X in Madison Square Garden in March 1994, a Bill Clinton impersonator appeared. Ted DiBiase told him that he had to agree that everyone has a price for the Million Dollar Man. An on-screen internal revenue agent named Irwin R. Shyster, or IRS, said that he'd worked out a deal with Clinton and he congratulated him on raising the taxes. Just a couple of weeks later, the WWF was proud to feature the real Bill and Hillary

Clinton on its programming as the WWF had been invited to participate in the annual White House Easter egg hunt. Doink the Clown and the Bushwackers were present.

In November 1995, another Bill Clinton impersonator appeared and sat in the front row for the Survivor Series in Landover, Maryland and he was good for a few yucks. Clinton mixed up Bam Bam Bigelow for Bam Bam from the *Flinstones* cartoon, allowing the WWF's Todd Pettengill to retort with " . . . and they say *your* administration is out of touch." To drive home Clinton's coquettish reputation, a WWF valet, Tammy Sytch, known as Sunny to fans, was sitting in his lap, while he stared at her chest and they exchanged sexual innuendo. Bob Backlund asked him if he considered himself one of the 8,000 irrelevant employees of the federal government, to which Clinton replied that he had nothing else to do.

Bob Backlund had already declared his storyline run for President on a May 15, 1995 episode of Monday Night Raw. He stated firmly that he was contemplating a run for President. A brass band came out along with someone holding a "Mr. Backlund for President" sign. Future vignettes, in Backlund's typical ranting style, railed for things like increasing the work week from forty to sixty hours, ending all holidays, except his birthday and requiring that all music be classical. Most memorably,

Backlund told viewers that the vacation was over and it was time to get off the government dole.

In March 1997, Gov. Christie Todd Whitman of New Jersey deregulated professional wrestling and removed a tax on professional wrestling events. With the Undertaker, in full wrestling garb, the jokes about burying the tax and regulation were plentiful. Linda McMahon explained how the tax had prevented previous major events from disseminating from the state in the past. One of the company's most prestigious events, Summerslam, would emanate from the state in August.

When the WWF returned to Atlantic City in 1997 following the abolishment of the Media Tax Act, business was heating up as the company was entering the Attitude Era and new stars were emerging. Familiar faces from the Atlantic City WrestleManias on the August 18, 1997 edition of Monday Night Raw included Shawn Michaels and Bret Hart. With the setup staging needed for the program, an attendance of 8,672 was a sellout, drawing ticket revenue of $155,261.

Trump's business acumen would not serve him well for long. The Trump Taj Mahal, Trump Castle and Trump Plaza and Casino, or Trump's three Atlantic City hotels and casinos, all went bankrupt. Under the stock symbol DJT, Trump Hotels and Resort Casinos went public in 1995. In August of 2004, Trump's stake in Trump Hotels and Casino Resorts dropped from 56 percent to 25 percent as part of a Chapter 11 bankruptcy to restructure $1.8 million in debt. Following attempts at restructuring, bankruptcy and sale, Trump Plaza closed permanently in September 2016. Trump was no longer the owner and had filed a lawsuit that his name be removed.

Over the last two decades, Atlantic City has been a fairly quiet town for WWE cards. From 1998-2012, only eight WWF/WWE shows were run there, a very small number considering the company's base in the northeastern United States. However, six of those eight shows were televised events. Upstart rival and loosely affiliated business partner Extreme Championship Wrestling came to town for a house show event on August 28, 1998. They drew a disappointing 500 fans at the Armory, a Trump owned facility this was not, and did not return before closing shop; ECW was later acquired by WWE in 2001. From 2013 on, Atlantic City has picked up to a once- or twice-a-year tour stop for WWE. There were five WWE wrestling shows run between 2013–2016, none of which were televised.

3 RAW: HYPING THE BATTLE OF THE BILLIONAIRES

I believe non-politicians represent the wave of the future, and if elected, I would make the kind of President America needs in the new millennium.

Donald Trump (1999)

Someone marries a hot chick; Trump gets divorced and marries a hotter one.

Vince McMahon (2007)

In the years between Trump's highest profile WrestleMania appearances, he would have several notable interactions with his WrestleMania IV acquaintance, Jesse "The Body" Ventura. Trump appeared at a campaign event supporting Ventura's run for Governor of Minnesota. Ventura's eventual win in 1998 was described as tens of thousands of voters tuning in late, supporting a third-party candidate and rejecting traditional choices. Young people were encouraged to make their voices heard.

Ventura, in his book, *I Ain't Got Time to Bleed*, described the dim outlook on his prospects when he decided to run: "Everybody thought it was a great joke: the big ex-pro wrestler running for governor- what's he gonna do, body-slam legislators when they get out of line?" The press barely noticed, according to Ventura.

Dean Barkley was the man who convinced Ventura to run for office. Barkley formed the Minnesota Reform Party in 1992, after being inspired by Ross Perot and ran unsuccessfully for a House seat and two runs at the Senate. While walking in a Fourth of July parade, Barkley was surprised to see the positive reception Ventura received that he described as the "Ventura Mystique," even though it was Barkley's hometown. Through persistence, Barkley convinced Ventura to attend the 1997 Minnesota State Fair as a representative of the Reform Party and received another positive response. Barkley became chairman of his campaign.

Ventura declared his candidacy on January 26, 1998, by announcing at the Minnesota State Capitol steps, "If I fail . . . then the American dream is dead." There was no opposition to an endorsement from the Reform Party and he officially accepted at their convention. While candidates spoke of various measures to control the budget, Ventura broke it down simply, "Cut taxes. Cut taxes. Cut taxes." In meeting with veterans in a legion hall, Ventura confidently shared that he was "going to fool everybody in this race like I fooled them on the one in Brooklyn Park ... Look, 45 percent of Minnesotans don't vote- and we're in a good state. I can get 20 percent of them to vote this one time and watch your vote count."

Ventura returned to the Minnesota State fair in 1998, now with an official purpose. His booth was swamped with swarms of people that wanted to get a "Ventura for Governor" bumper sticker and a 'Retaliate in '98" t-shirt. The t-shirts were especially popular during the campaign, raising $150,000 of the $300,000 total raised in the campaign. Jacob Lentz, author of *Electing Jesse Ventura*, described Ventura as "radiating pure populism" when making statements like "I don't believe in politics, I believe in results." Most fair goers were more interested in meeting Ventura for entertainment value. Campaign representatives were passing out "Jesse Dollars," with Ventura's face replacing Washington's. The fair also gave Ventura the opportunity to rebrand himself with reporters: "I make my living with my mind now, not my body so I'm Jesse 'The Mind.'"

Part of Ventura's strategy was to appeal to the non-voter. If 50 percent of the population did not vote in non-presidential elections, that was a potential supporter he could attract, who had no compulsion to vote democrat or republican.

A breakthrough for Ventura included the use of creative television advertisements. Bill Hillman, who ran an advertising firm in Minnesota, liked populists and noticed the interest Ventura had received at the State Fair. He contacted Barkley to join the campaign and was surprised to learn there was not much of a strategy. The campaign also had only one staffer, no fax machine and could not pay to run a poll. Hillman had ideas: "I thought he had a great appeal to what some people would call Reagan Democrats or blue-collar Democrats." Hillman explained to Ventura, "If you're going to run as a Populist, you're only going to have one shot. The press will never treat you like they do the first time."

Even with an advertising person helping to steer the ship, the campaign had cash troubles and did not have the funding for tv commercials. The campaign's first radio ad used the music from the movie, Shaft: "While the other guys were cashing checks, he was in the navy getting dirty and wet." Once able to run an advertisement, the ads aired on programs that would appeal to younger people, like The Simpsons and Saturday Night Live, a Ventura action figure took center stage to fight Evil Special Interest Man. Ventura's campaign qualified for $360,000 in public money. This allowed it to run advertisements during the last week of the campaign.

The statewide debates were the time when Ventura's candidacy heated up and the agreement among observers was that Ventura had won all six. Ventura often was vague but had phrases that would resonate such as "With freedom comes responsibility, but I prefer freedom and I think people will show the responsibility." In addition to his well-honed verbal jousting skills, Ventura felt his physical prowess and towering height over his less athletic opponents served a benefit.

The Pioneer Press bought what Ventura was selling. On October 26, it featured a headline, "Ventura's straight talk merits respect." On October 28, the paper wrote that Ventura is incapable of deception. For a third-party candidate, Ventura benefitted overall from a good deal of press. Ventura received about half of the mentions in the major papers, The Star Tribune and the Pioneer Press, as compared to his rivals. In a content analysis, Jacob Lentz found a positive depiction of Ventura personally and as a candidate. He benefited from little scrutiny and limited investigation of claims by the press.

On Election Night, Knight Ridder newspapers described supporters behind Ventura as white males under 30 years old, wearing t-shirts with wrestling logos like

NWO (New World Order). Outside of Ventura's election night location, he was asked several times to request his supporters calm down as spontaneous moshing kept breaking out. His campaign people kept requesting his help: "Jesse, the kids are getting wild again. You gotta go out there and talk to 'em, calm 'em down." Ventura had "tapped into the vast demographics of pro wrestling" and more than 50 percent of Ventura's voters were males under 44, many of them first time voters. Chuck Raasch, in the Daily Record of New Jersey, warned that what happened in Minnesota could happen anywhere. Stephen M. Layden (Lake George, NY) in a letter to the editor in the Post Star wrote, "I have seen the future of politics . . . its name is pro wrestling." Often getting little mention in stories noting Ventura's win was his previous experience in politics.

37 percent of voters selected Ventura in a three-way win. One benefit to Ventura was same day registrants. Of those 332,540 who registered the day of the election, 225,184 voted for Ventura. Overall Ventura received 48.5 percent among those 18-29 years old but he also received strong support among those 30–44 years old at 42.9 percent.

Although Ventura was likely wealthy at the time, he appealed to groups on the lower end of the socioeconomic scale by portraying himself as an outsider and hero to blue collar workers; his "dude" persona arguably contributed to his success. Ventura knew how to appeal to this group, including his status as a union member (albeit the Actors Guild union). He could communicate in an informal, straight talk manner. As shared in *Electing Jesse Ventura*, if one utilizes the 1998 Voter News Service Poll and defines "dudes" as men with a high school education or less, and less than $50,000 a year in earnings. Ventura received 48.2 percent support, compared to men earning $75,000 a year and had at least a college degree, where Ventura only received 30.3 percent.

Jacob Lentz warns that because someone does not understand something (like professional wrestling), it does not make it less legitimate. To dismiss a candidate immediately because of a less respectable biography could be foolish. Many find pro wrestling to be a poor representation of American culture but for others, and great numbers of them at that time, it was a legitimate form of culture and how people want to spend their free time.

When Ventura became Governor, the WWF was happy to celebrate in a press release: "The World Wrestling Federation is proud that one of its own, Jesse 'the Body' Ventura, has been elected Governor of Minnesota. Vince

McMahon takes full credit for teaching Jesse Ventura the finer art of bullshit! . . . not only is there life after WWF, we can only ask what next? Steve Austin for President!?" Michael Kazin, in the Tampa Bay Times, argued that Ventura was miscategorized as a Populist, but his closest roots were to a fellow outsider, Ross Perot. Ventura claimed he wanted to destroy the property tax system and reduce the role of government. Kazin felt his political ideology landed closest to Libertarian.

On ABC's This Week on December 20, 1998, Donald Trump, Governor Ventura and Presidential hopeful Steve Forbes were on to talk about presidential politics, the Reform Party and the World Trade Organization.

Despite past estrangement between the WWF and Jesse Ventura, by the summer of 1999, Governor Ventura was back in the WWF fold. On July 12, 1999, Ventura announced a forthcoming press conference with the wrestling organization on Wednesday. Ventura, while saying charities would benefit, did not yet make it clear whether he'd be returning to the ring as a wrestler (something he had not done since 1986) or referee. Wrestling pundits, Dave Meltzer and Wade Keller, speculated the event could gross $20 million and Ventura could earn around $1 million. Ventura would later say that he would receive $100,000, half would go to the Jade Foundation for Disadvantaged Children, named in honor of his daughter, and the other half would endow a scholarship at his alma mater, Roosevelt High School. He also hoped to donate to Make-A-Wish Foundation. Ventura would also receive proceeds for the use of his name in promotion and according to Ventura, "a normal percentage" of a royalty on videotape sales (a matter of disagreement during Ventura's last stint with the company in which Ventura received an estimated $1 million according to the Star Tribune), but he would not disclose figures or where that money would ultimately end up.

The WWF released a statement that Ventura would "return to the ring" at Summerslam in Minnesota's Target Center. While the live event had already sold out, the publicity was expected to help pay-per-view sales. The Governor planned his vacation time to participate. Before his role was even announced, Ventura was on the defensive in justifying his participation: "The perception is that people need to be professional politicians and that therefore being a politician is your entire life. Well, it's not Jesse Ventura's entire life and I think I was elected upon the fact that I came from being a private citizen."

"There's no rule that the governor can't have fun. There's no rule that says a governor on his own can't be a human." Ventura told CNN's Wolf Blitzer.

He also felt that his affiliation with Summerslam would bring greater visibility to Minnesota state: "More people will see Minnesota again and it will put us in the spotlight again." The event had a slogan: "Out of Body Experience," a takeoff on Ventura's original wrestling nickname. Minnesota GOP Chairman Ron Eibensteiner described Ventura's actions as "an absolute outrage."

At that Wednesday's press conference, Jesse Ventura, wearing a feather boa and sunglasses and "projecting an aura of respectable authority" according to the *Star Tribune*, confirmed the speculation: at Summerslam, he would be a referee and return law and order back to wrestling. Turning to Vince McMahon, Ventura said: "I'm more powerful than you. I'm more powerful than the World Wrestling Federation. As long as you're in the state, you hold no power here. It's very simple. It's The Body rules, it's my rules or the highway." Sean Waltman, a Minnesota native and member of the WWF's D-Generation X faction, warmed up the crowd of 1,000 at the press conference. Wearing a t-shirt with the catchphrase "Suck it" on the front. Waltman said that he had two words for politicians and other people who looked down at professional wrestling fans, then proceeded to point and chop at his crotch.

When it was McMahon's turn, he said that "there is nothing going on in the World Wrestling Federation that hasn't gone on in the White House." Reporters who questioned how the Governor could justify his participation were shouted down by fans in the audience.

Representative Al Junkhe was disappointed that the announcement took attention away from the funeral for Representative William Munger, a Democrat from Duluth. Senator Dean Johnson, a Republican representing Willmar, met with Minnesota National Guard Troops and reported that they were disappointed in Ventura's decision: "He would be so good at calling attention to problems rather than calling attention to himself."

David Schultz, President of Common Cause Minnesota filed a conflict of interest complaint against Governor Ventura with the Department of Employee Relations. There was concern that the Governor's official position was being used to obtain privileges and benefits that are not available to the general public. Schultz said that his "independence of judgement" related to matters that affect the WWF and the state.

Ventura would participate in an opportunity to promote the forthcoming pay-per-view on Monday Night Raw in Chicago on August 9, 1999. Ventura flew from St. Louis, where he was attending the National Governors

Association meeting, to Chicago, and then back to St. Louis the same night. Ventura's spokesperson assured the *Star Tribune* that Ventura's participation would come at no additional costs, including a flight for Ventura and his two security guards.

On Sunday, August 22, Jesse Ventura performed in his role as referee in the main event of Summerslam, overseeing Stone Cold Steve Austin defend his title against HHH and Mankind, Mick Foley. 78 media representatives were in attendance for a form of entertainment that often slips under the radar, even during its peak periods. There was a backstage skit between Mankind and Ventura:
Mankind: "Don't you think Geraldine Ferraro was an underrated candidate?"
Ventura: "She might have been but she was a bleeding-heart liberal."

Ventura took the microphone when he entered the ring: "Let me tell you something. There's a lot of media saying I'm a disgrace for being here. But let me tell you, I'm proud I'm a wrestler and I'm proud I was a wrestler and I'm proud to be here." The crowd cheered. Mankind won the belt but what was most notable to the media was the Governor's language:
To Chyna: "Get your ass out of the ring."
To Shane McMahon: "Don't you come out here and tell

me shit" and "That's one for your old man, you little bastard."

Deanna Ross, a childcare provider, attended the event and provided a brief interview to the *Star Tribune*. She said it was Sunday and he could do what he wants on his day off. She didn't have concerns about Ventura upholding the dignity of office: "We've got a president who's having sex with interns, Jesse's making money? So what? Isn't that the American way?"

Ventura's business manager, David Olsen, said that there has been casual conversations about a return but nothing concrete. Olsen said the WWF felt Ventura had done a good job and it'd be nice to have him back at some point.

Hulk Hogan declared his candidacy for President in 2000. Appearing on *The Tonight Show* with Jay Leno in 1998, Hogan announced that he was retiring from wrestling to run for office.

The *Los Angeles Daily News* wrote to forget Jesse Ventura as that was small time compared to Hogan running for President. Hogan said: "People are ready for a change. Everybody has a bit of good in them, even the worst criminals." Hogan's mother-in-law at the time was supportive of his run: "Certainly to stay on top as long as he has takes a great deal of business and personal ethics."

Forgetting Hogan's promotional affiliations at that time, Robert Hertzberg, a Democratic California Assemblyman, stated that "The way things are going, the World Wrestling Federation is going to have to register as a political party." The paper reported that straw polls in Tampa (Hogan's place of residence) showed that Hogan would win a presidential race against Al Gore or Jeb Bush. Why the poll did not include the actual Bush that ran, and won the presidency, was not clear.

Jesse Ventura was skeptical of Hogan's serious interest in the race: "I have long since left professional wrestling. He is still in it. That's hype they do simply for pro wrestling." Hogan's retirement lasted for just one month. It would have been especially odd to go ahead with a campaign as Hogan was coasting during the final peak of Ted Turner's World Championship Wrestling, and earning big bucks as his contract entitled him to twenty-five percent of all pay-per-view revenues in which he appeared.

In late 1999, the WWF began naming a handful of Board Members to its company. In addition to Vince and Linda McMahon and company CEO August Liguori, Lowell Weicker Jr. was one of those outside the company named. Weicker had served as Connecticut Governor through 1995. As a board member, Weicker would receive $25,000 per year and an option to purchase 25,000 shares.

Trump next attended a WWF show at Madison Square Garden in 2000, by which time he had moved on to a new love interest. Melania Knauss (born Melanija Knavs), the future Mrs. Melania Trump, sat ringside for the night with her then boyfriend. Trump was divorced from Marla Maples in 1999.

In a moment captioned "Donald, Duck!" in print, Trump and Melania may have had more action than they bargained for. Wrestler David Heath, known as Gangrel, was playing a vampire character. As part of his gimmick, he would drink a liquid resembling blood from a goblet and then spew it in the air with the remnants falling on the audience that was in his path. The photo caption described the moment in this way: "Tycoon Donald Trump and girlfriend Melania Knauss got an up-close and personal look at Gangrel's entrance at a recent Madison Square Garden show. Gangrel's mysterious red mist sent 'The Donald' and Melania scrambling for cover!"

In this instance, Trump may not have been wise to obtain the best seats. Melania looks surprised or frightened in the picture while Trump seems to be enjoying the moment. Trump's children have attended shows with him following this incident but Melania has not returned.

Gangrel and Trump do share one thing in

common, besides an interest in professional wrestling: both have been married three times, thus far.

By 2000, another all-time great, "Nature Boy" Ric Flair, was considering a run for Governorship, this one in North Carolina. Flair went to meet with Ventura when he travelled to St. Paul. "I'm definitely inspired by his success," said Flair. Flair was considering running as an independent and told Regis and Kathie Lee he was dead serious. Flair said "I may have to tone down a few things, but I think charisma can go a long way." Over the years, there have been several stories of Flair flashing his penis in public without warning, such as when he flashed a stewardess on a WWE-chartered trip returning from Europe, as noted by Rob Wolkenbrod in an article on *Fansided* describing the numerous incidents on the trip.; it's fair to argue Flair would have had to tone things down.

The Reform Party was considering Donald Trump for the 2000 presidential ticket. Trump and Ventura held a press conference in Brooklyn Park, Minnesota during an action-packed day that included a variety of fundraisers and were coy about its purpose and their aims. The Associated Press reported Trump was considering a $100 million dollar run for President and it was thought that Ventura would endorse him. Trump told the AP that only death would prevent him from running.

In regard to Ventura in speaking with reporters on his plane ride over, Trump said, "I think if I decide to run he will endorse me . . . If I decide to run, I feel I have a very good chance of getting Jesse's endorsement." Ventura said, "When Donald announces his candidacy, ask me then."

A reporter questioned Trump as to why he had been so sure of Ventura's endorsement previously and Trump denied it: "I didn't say that, when did I say that?" Trump attributed it to the reporter being from the *New York Post*. Ventura was courting Trump for the Reform Party, to stave off Pat Buchanan's chances as Ventura considered Buchanan too conservative as compared to Trump. Trump listened as Ventura said, "To show you how fraudulent voting can be, never, not once, was I polled to be the winner." Ventura in discussing presidential strategy wanted to be part of a party that is centrist and too far to the left or to the right wasn't a winning combination.

At the same time, there was speculation that Ventura would himself run for President. Ventura was hoping for support from the WWF in launching a run, but Vince McMahon never responded to his proposal. Ventura suggested a storyline idea where Vince McMahon would be running for President (in storyline only) and Ventura would be his on-screen rival and boost his exposure for an actual run.

Trump and Ventura felt a certain kinship of being "self-made men." Trump said, "there's a big difference between creating a lot of wealth and being a member of the lucky sperm club, which a number of different people that are running right now are," in a dig that included George W. Bush. Trump felt he did not fall into that category given his father's wealth since he had to rebuild his wealth. In the lobby, both men had what is referred to in wrestling as "gimmick tables." Trump had copies of his latest book for sale, "*The America We Deserve*" and Ventura had action figures for $22, reportedly for charity.

Due to the success of outsider candidates like Ventura, Trump's flirtation with the Presidency was getting attention, like when he shared the cover of *Newsweek* with Ventura and Warren Beatty. Ventura got the main billing on the cover that day. In forming an exploratory committee in October 1999, he listed his poll numbers as "unbelievable," when in fact it had been reflecting 7 percent support.

In a *Newsweek* poll, Trump was last among 12 actual or potential candidates. Mike Murphy, a Republican strategist, would not mind if Trump did not run: "I think the voters would rather get back to the issues rather than this story about whether the New York billionaire can beat the former pro wrestler to become the third-party nominee who won't win anyway." Neal Gabler, an author focused on the power of celebrity, said that "A Donald, A Jesse Ventura, play to this idea that politics is just another form of entertainment, and the spoils go to the individual who puts on the best show." Deborah Mathis summed up the appeal of Trump and Ventura in her article title from *Tribune News Services*: "Americans hunger for truth. How else to explain the babble of Ventura, Trump?"

Trump and Ventura also had a notable meal together at Trump International Hotel in 1999. They were joined by a movie star, Woody Harrelson at the two-and-a-half-hour meal. The trio was described as leaving the location arm in arm by the *Star Tribune*. Ventura said humorously that "Mr. Trump and I did a lot of discussing tonight at dinner and we decided that Woody is going to be the next President of the United States." Ventura looked at the gathered crowd and gave a general "No comment" while Trump responded to a question about running for President, "Yeah, I am." Years later, Harrelson would reflect upon the experience: "It was brutal, it was brutal." Harrelson went on that "I never met a more narcissistic man." Doug Friedline, a political strategist who was known for "favoring the underdog," was partially credited with Ventura's rise to Governor. He later assisted

Trump when he explored the possibility of a run for President. He also tried, unsuccessfully to recruit Bruce Springsteen to run for Senate. Friedline was found dead in his home in November 2006 at the age of 49.

Donald Trump wanted to know how Ventura did it. In a two-hour meeting in the Northland Inn in Brooklyn Park, Minnesota, Barkley and Ventura met with Trump. They broke down their successful campaign strategy month by month including use of media and money. They explained their anti-establishment approach and the "Retaliate in '98" strategy.

Initiated by Linda McMahon in July 2000, the WWF had been actively involved in a "non-partisan" effort to register young voters to participate in the election process through the Smackdown Your Vote!! campaign. Television time was devoted over several months to encourage fans to vote. According to the Smackdown Your Vote! campaign, just exercise your right to vote. After all, per the website, the mission was to "encourage young people to become active participants in their democracy and vote." At certain points, high school "ambassadors" were recruited for a chance to win a $2,000 scholarship (and was soon hoping to extend its reach to college campuses). The goal was listed as "simple": "register as many college students as possible." Part of the draw was a potential visit from a WWE Superstar to one's campus. 150,000 voters were registered in the first year.

Dwayne 'the Rock' Johnson attended the Republican National Convention in 2000. He was given a speaking slot in the wrestling stronghold of Philadelphia, PA and even introduced the Speaker of the House Dennis Hastert as an "honorable" former amateur wrestling coach. (It would not be until 2016 that Hastert was sentenced to fifteen-months in jail for performing bank transactions in an effort to cover up sexual abuse of young boys on the Illinois wrestling team he coached. The statute of limitations had expired on any potential charges related to sexual abuse). Hastert said that the Rock had registered to vote that very week, and that young people should register to vote just like him. Later, he sat with George H.W. Bush.

The Rock was in attendance at the behest of WWE as part of the Smackdown Your Vote! campaign (Linda McMahon was in attendance with him). The Rock assured interviewers that WWE did not portray murder or rape. The C-Span commentator, Steve Scully, stated that he had no idea who the Rock was. When the Rock said that viewers knew what he was cooking, Scully awkwardly asked him what he was cooking. The Rock came out to his entrance music and remained in character: "Let me get this straight. You invited the Rock to the Republican National Convention?"

At the Democratic National Convention, Chyna and The Rock debuted public service announcements for Smackdown Your Vote! the first time PSA's had been made outside of WWF television.

The WWF invited Al Gore and George W. Bush to have five minutes each to speak on Smackdown in the run up to the Presidential election in 2000 in a "Smackdown Challenge." That summer, the WWF had registered 40,000 voters as part of the Smackdown Your Vote! campaign. Mick Foley, serving as the WWF's Commissioner at the time, invited the candidates to "speak directly to the youth of America." Jesse Ventura was invited to moderate the discussion. Linda McMahon said that "We have a wonderful forum to reach out to them . . . You have to have a sense of fun. You have to have a little humor in the campaign as well." The campaigns told the media that they were reviewing the invitation to debate. Neither candidate did appear.

According to the *Los Angeles Times*, Smackdown Your Vote! helped the company to curry favor with Republicans, as that is the party that the company's fans support, according to Gary Davis. "And what could be more ideal than doing voter registration in a Presidential election year? We wanted to represent our fans: Middle America." It was a win for all when the Rock participated in the RNC and Davis attributes it to interesting fans in politics.

A table for registering volunteers on behalf of Smackdown Your Vote! in Hartford had not yet perfected their pitch: 'Vote, vote, vote"; "The Rock says to vote"; "Stone Cold says to vote."

The Baltimore Sun reported that volunteers set up their tables at 6:00 p.m. but there was already a lack of Smackdown Your Vote! t-shirts. The volunteers were offered shirts with "Come get some" on the back, which was said to have made some uncomfortable.

Bob Backlund helped to draw fans to the table in support of his run for Senate. He yelled, "Register to vote!" while signing autographs as well as "Smackdown your vote!." 83 voters were registered that day at the event.

WWE commentator and Memphis regional main eventer, Jerry Lawler would test the political waters, running unsuccessfully for Mayor of Memphis in 1999, earning just over 11 percent of the votes. His strategy included pursuing the youth vote and finding people who normally did not follow politics or government to vote for him. Although Lawler brought a good deal of local name recognition, it did not carry him too far. Lawler's greatest impact on the political landscape took place on Monday Night Raw on November 6, 2000. With WWE's most popular program running on Monday nights, it is always well positioned to leave a lasting influence with swing voters the night before an election.

The night before the hotly contested election between Bush and Gore in 2000, the WWF revealed its true hand. During a matchup between the Hardy Boyz (Jeff & Matt), a popular young free-spirited team that many fans looked up to, and Right to Censor, an oppressive, overbearing group in button down shirts and ties, Lawler was provided the opportunity to compare Right to Censor to Al Gore and running mate, Joseph Lieberman. In a contrived exchange, Jim Ross asked Jerry Lawler who he was going to vote for. It seems like Lawler hesitated a moment and it was hard to hear him. Ross asked him again who he would be voting for. Lawler's confidence now grew, and he said he was not going to be voting for Gore-Lieberman as they could be card-carrying members of the Right to Censor because they love to censor things (naturally). Ross reminded viewers that "The King's" views were his own, but qualified to say that it does not mean he was voting for Gore-Lieberman either. Lawler then stated he was voting for Bush and reminded viewers they are in Texas (Houston, specifically).

To be clear, Vince McMahon, since stepping back a few years previously as the lead play-by-play announcer, whose style would often come across as hokey and cartoonish to long-time fans, was now producing Monday Night Raw from backstage. McMahon would regularly emphasize points that he wanted the announcers to make via headset.

The next day would yield one of the closest presidential elections in history with only 537 votes separating the candidates in the decisive state of Florida. With millions of viewers at home, could Lawler have influenced 500–600 fans to go to the polls and vote for Bush? It is hard to say. WWE would be participating in an event to celebrate George W. Bush's inauguration in Washington, D.C. Kurt and Debra Angle would be on hand to celebrate that Friday night at Club Insomnia, where they would meet and dance with fans. Gary Davis said, "This is our way of supporting this process." Governor Ventura, The Rock and Chyna had also been invited to attend. Tickets costed $350—one of the least expensive events in D.C. that week.

Former WWWF champion Bob Backlund cast a ballot for the first time in 1996. He explained that he "was one of those people who didn't care for the political arena." Backlund later ran for political office himself in

2000 in his home state of Connecticut, inspired by Jesse Ventura: "I thought Ventura's win was one of the greatest things that ever happened in our business, the business of wrestling." Backlund acquired a red Chevrolet Nova for his "mobile office."

Linda McMahon endorsed Backlund: "I can certainly tell you I think Bob is as qualified as many of the people I've seen running for office, and more qualified as many of the people sitting in congress today."

While the odds had been long to win a First District seat against Democratic congressman John Larson, Backlund was not dissuaded by the long odds: "I like uphill battles." Backlund struggled to answer questions at debates and as reported by the *Hartford Courant*: "Backlund sometimes looks lost and searches for an answer as if he has not considered his position on the issue."

Michele Jacklin, the *Hartford Courant*'s political columnist, took a critical view of Backlund's candidacy, while seeming to take a liking to Backlund as a person: "It's hard to understand why Backlund is running for Congress other than he possibly needs a job and Republican Party leaders thought he'd be a novelty. If so, they've perpetrated a cruel hoax and shamelessly exploited a man who seems decent and kind and big-hearted."

Backlund's campaign materials included promotional photos from his time as the WWWF champion. His business cards had the following: "PLEASE VOTE. Bob Backlund. I will increase my ability to READ." Backlund actually taught himself to read later in life, despite receiving a degree from North Dakota State University and being nearly illiterate at the time. Backlund's campaign purchased an advertisement to air on local cable during Monday Night Raw. It costs $112 to air and nothing to produce. Wearing a red bow tie and suspenders, Backlund's television ads consisted of him red faced and yelling into a handheld camera, wearing a clip on microphone: "We are bigger than you are and we are going to win whether you like it or not." Backlund challenged his opponent, John Larsen: "Let's get back in the arena and fight, young man." Larsen was flattered as he is one year older than Backlund.

Other advertisements were of a more serious nature. In one, Backlund stands in manure while a horse nibbles on his ear and says that he will not make promises like other politicians. Seth Rosenblit, Backlund's campaign publicist, said that "If 14- and 15-year-olds could vote, guys like Bob would be President of the United States."

Kan Dautrich of the University of Connecticut's Center for Survey Research and Analysis said that the problem with Backlund is that, "in this environment, voters are not looking for change. They want the status quo."

He raised $80,000 (including selling t-shirts at WWE live events) compared with Larsen's $600,000. John Kohut, Senior Editor of the *Rothenberg Political Report*, said Republicans were counting on "the flamboyance factor." For a man whose main attribute was his in-ring acumen for the first part of his career, they'd apparently picked the wrong wrestler; Backlund lost the race.

Jesse Ventura would reconnect with Vince McMahon in the form of a WWF owned property by late 2000: the XFL.

The XFL was the company's failed attempt at challenging the National Football League, run as a co-partnership with NBC. The league got off to a strong rating start on NBC on a Saturday night but hit record ratings lows within a few weeks. The hype of what the league would be was not matched in the amateurish athletics taking place on the screen. WWE and NBC each lost $35 million dollars on the venture. Vince McMahon said the XFL would be the "people's league." McMahon continued that "the NFL abandoned me along with the rest of Middle America."

Ventura served as on-air analyst for the XFL,

similar to his role as a color commentator for WWF years ago. He was not being thrown into a completely new world: He'd served as an analyst for Tampa Bay Buccaneers broadcasts in 1989 and 1990, as well as a season for the Minnesota Vikings in 1991.

The XFL season would run from February 3 until April 7, 2001 with Ventura committed to twelve Saturday games. *The Pioneer Press* estimated Ventura could earn between $250,000 to $1 million for a season's work.

Ventura had a complaint filed against him at around this time. He was accused of being in violation of ethics laws as a state employee. The relevant law states that a conflict of interest arises when outside work could interfere in official duties. Moe cited the Vikings request for a new stadium and an XFL job as a potential conflict. Ventura did his best to assuage any fears: "In my contract with the XFL, it's clear that if at any time my governor duties are such that I can't make it, that's fully accepted by the league and NBC. Being Governor comes first and I don't see it as any major problem." Julien Carter, Commissioner of the Department of Employer Relations, and recently instilled in the position by Ventura, issued a statement that Ventura's job with the XFL did not constitute a conflict of interest.

Ventura's contract allowed him to miss XFL

games at his discretion, but for each of the games missed, his earnings would be reduced. The contract stated that Ventura's role as Governor could not be mentioned in any way in promoting the league. It didn't take long for the XFL to violate this provision. In an advertisement in late 2000, language included the following: "As the nation waits for its next President, the XFL is declaring Jesse (the Governor) Ventura the new color commentator of the XFL."

Critics were ready to pounce on Ventura and the XFL. Ventura's performance as a color commentator (while sitting in the stands) was graded a C– from USA Today's Rudy Martzke. Richard Sandomir of the *New York Times* described Ventura's performance as a "roaring river of inanities." Steve Johnson of the *Chicago Tribune* wrote that "listening to the broadcast was like having Jesse Ventura berate you for three hours." Johnson wrote that Ventura was less entertaining than Dennis Miller on Monday Night Football.

The game was exciting until halftime, though both teams went scoreless in the second half. Producers remembered not to mention that Ventura was a sitting Governor. The ratings for the first show on NBC were strong, especially in the Minnesota market, but then dropped off significantly from week to week. In a sign that the league may have been snake bitten, Ventura was off the air for forty-six minutes due to a power failure at the Los Angeles Coliseum on the second week's broadcast. Each week flirted with new lows for a broadcast network and quickly became the butt of jokes to many.

By mid-March, Vince McMahon looked to play the blame game for ratings that had debuted with a 10.3 but dropped to a 2.7, and Jesse Ventura was in his sights. He described Ventura as being on thin ice and said one of the league's biggest mistakes was its selection of broadcasters given the Governor's closer connection to pro wrestling than the world of football. McMahon said that research the league conducted showed he was too over the top for fan's liking. There was speculation that McMahon was trying to get Ventura to quit so he didn't have to pay out the remaining terms of his contract. State representative Phil Krinkie, who had criticized Ventura for his moonlighting thought that it could benefit the state of Minnesota if Ventura had more time to concentrate on issues like the budget. Chris Gilbert, a Political Science Professor at Gustavus Adolphus College was quoted in the *Star Tribune*: "The XFL has been a disaster and the sooner he gets it behind him, the better."

By April, McMahon was walking back some of his harsh criticism: "I think Jesse was unfairly criticized by a lot of people, myself included. He made a lot of contributions and was very supportive of the league, in spite of the media jumping down his throat. He wasn't brought in for his football knowledge, although he does know football. The mistake we made was not putting a football expert in with Jesse in the first place."

The first iteration of the XFL would be dead shortly after the season concluded, leaving the WWF and the NBC with some heavy losses and embarrassment. Ventura wouldn't have to worry about concerns of his moonlighting or being blamed for any future failures. An Our Perspective editorial in the *Star Tribune*, titled "eX-FL", perhaps summed it up best: "From its first Saturday night. The XFL disappointed football fans, wrestling fans and Ventura fans alike."

Despite the public posturing, it would not be long before Ventura appeared on WWF programming again. Jesse Ventura appeared on screen at the Target Center on June 4, 2001. He also "overruled" Vince McMahon's authority and provided fans what they wanted: A match between champion Stone Cold Steve Austin and challenger, Chris Jericho.

While the world was not immune to the effects of the tragic events of September 11, 2001, it seemed to reawaken a particularly passionate calling in Vince

McMahon and through his primary bullhorn: WWE, . The company proudly claimed to host the first public gathering after 9/11, and emanating from Texas, McMahon gave a speech that the spirit of America lives in Houston, which elicited loud cheers from the audience.

Stephanie McMahon framed the event in another tragedy that she could understand: When the government put her father on trial for steroid distribution allegations.

Vince and Linda McMahon decided to donate one million dollars to the New York Relief Funds, which would consist of half from the WWF and half directly from the McMahon's. Office staff raised an additional $32,000. When they came to New York, personnel visited fire stations and Ground Zero.

Linda McMahon explained in late October that Monday night program would change from *Raw is War* to *Raw* due to a sensitivity for the real conflicts occurring in the world at the time.

In 2002, the World Wrestling Federation was forced to change its name. Back in 1994, it reached an agreement with the World Wide Fund for Nature, a wildlife organization founded in 1961 that shared its initials. The agreement said the wrestling company could still use "WWF" when referring to themselves on broadcasts but would stop using the acronym in other situations, such as on advertising, in promoting upcoming events, or on merchandise like t-shirts and baseball caps. In return, Titan Sports would continue using "World Wrestling Federation" on their logo.

The conservation group later took the wrestling promotion to court and received an injunction—upheld on appeal—that forced the wrestling promotion to stick to the letter of the agreement. The company decided to change its name to WWE, short for World Wrestling Entertainment. The name change was announced in a brand-awareness campaign called "Get the F Out."

A marketing period known as "The Attitude Era," roughly from 1997–2002; it was time reposition. The company had transitioned from a family-friendly brand and was now marketed as trash TV, with nudity, swearing, sex and other lowbrow tactics to draw attention. "Stone Cold" Steve Austin and Dwayne "The Rock" Johnson emerged as stars from this period.

One step below those megastars was McMahon's future son-in-law, Paul Levesque, a wrestler better known as "Triple H." He benefited from looser censorship reins in by cursing, asking women to lift their shirts and making jokes related to genitalia. This style of television eventually ran its course, though. Fans grew tired of shock television and the ratings eventually dropped. The company had fallen into another lull after the conclusion of their proclaimed Attitude Era in 2002.

John Cena, a family friendly hero and modern-day stand-in for Hulk Hogan, served as poster child of the post-Attitude era. Cena could only take the brand so far on his shoulders, though, and ratings and pay-per-views turned stagnant.

Smackdown Your Vote! continued chugging along throughout 2001. When WWE kicked off a voting campaign aimed at high school students, Kurt Angle served as its honorary chairman. He often spoke at high schools corresponding with WWE television tapings.

In May, Angle visited Hartford High School. He was joined by Connecticut Secretary of State Susan Bysiewicz. When Smackdown Your Vote! held a gathering in June in front of the Capital building in Minnesota, the crowd of forty was so small that the crowd wasn't shown on television.

John "Bradshaw" Layfield, later a conservative news regular and purported locker room bully, and "Coach" Jonathan Coachman, a WWE commentator who later moved back to sports commentary at ESPN), kicked off the 2002's first Smackdown Your Vote! campaign on Monday, April 8 at Sunnyslope High School in Phoenix, Arizona with Secretary of State Betsey Bayless. Alabama was one of 13 states participating in the campaign in 2002. Secretary of State, Jim Bennett, was scheduled to speak with Kurt Angle as part of an effort to increase high school voter registration. Angelica Bridges of TV's *Baywatch* participated in the Smackdown Your Vote: Pledge to Participate tour in New York as part of the Summerslam festivities in the area.

In 2003, Florida State Representative Dave Aronberg, thirty-one years old, was named as one of three national chairpersons for Smackdown Your Vote. Aronberg, a wrestling fan, received a $500 campaign contribution from Linda McMahon. That year, WWE teamed up with the Hip-Hop Action Summit for the Smackdown Your Vote! campaign. Russell Simmons and Vince McMahon announced the team up. McMahon said at the press conference: "Wow. The WWE and hip-hop together—there goes the neighborhood, huh?." Rev. Run, of Run DMC, was excited: "I believe we're going to go more than double platinum."

Voter registration tables would appear both outside of wrestling and music venues. Gary Davis in the 40/40 Club's VIP room stated that "It's a good way to get to know each other. We'd love to do business with Russell."

John Layfield said their voting initiative was not

political: "America doesn't ask much but it does ask that you be involved." Maven Huffman, a WWE wrestler stressed the importance of every vote counting: "In the last Presidential election, Florida showed them how close an election could be."

The League of Women Voters, also involved in the initiative, was not concerned about WWE's racy storylines at the time. Kay Maxwell, the organization's president said: "In this case, they're serious about their goal. It's not a PR event from their perspective."

Olympic Gold Medalist and former WWE World Champion, Kurt Angle, served as the honorary co-chair in 2004 along with Bradshaw. The goal was to register a million more voters between 18 to 34-year old's in 2004, "A Million More in 2004." Linda McMahon characterized WWE as a "marketing company" in emphasizing the skills needed to reach voters. Ric Flair and Shawn Michaels were among the RNC participants. 4 million more young people voted in the national elections that year, for which the Smackdown Your Vote! campaign took partial credit.

"Whassup everybody? They told me to wear a suit and tie today, but this is the best I could do." John Cena attended a press conference in support of Smackdown Your Vote! in Washington, DC. He wore a chain around his neck, cutoff shorts and a Cleveland Cavaliers basketball jersey and said he felt he couldn't make his voice heard in 2000 so he declined to vote, but now understands the importance of voting. Bradshaw said, "Young people can swing this election if they choose to."

Smackdown Your Vote! was described as one of the more successful efforts to register youth voters. Nancy Worley, Alabama's Secretary of State was particularly impressed by seeing a school assembly go "bonkers" in Birmingham for the wrestlers: "Whatever turns them on, I say. If the wrestlers can motivate them, I'm with the wrestlers."

John Cena spoke at a Smackdown Your Vote! rally to encourage young people to vote in Lancaster, Ohio. At an event in the San Antonio Walmart, the Dallas Morning News reported that the age of those attending was closer to eight than eighteen. The wrestlers were inside signing autographs, and most were not talking politics, but Hillbilly Jim stressed the importance of voting to "safeguard our liberties."

House Minority Leader Nancy Pelosi invited WWE to participate in a youth summer on Capitol Hill in April, 2004. Pelosi was photographed giving a "headlock" to WWE Diva wrestler, Queen Victoria. The WWE asked President Bush and challenger Sen. John Kerry to complete a questionnaire on a number of issues that affect people between eighteen to thirty. The issues included the conflict in Iraq, education and the economy. Tara Kane of *The Record* said that both candidates had said it was important that young people vote, but neither gave a reason why and was not impressed with the following answers: "If elected, what will you do to make sure that the voices of year olds are heard and represented." Bush wrote about listening to the voices of the people and defeating terrorists while Kerry "would speak to the issues facing young Americans." WWE also issued a national voters issue pamphlet.

Linda McMahon, the Big Show and Ivory attended the 2004 Democratic convention. Big Show said, "I like politicians who don't dance around the Bush. 'Bush' as in shrub." Big Show and Mick Foley appeared at a Fleet Center event designed to appeal to young voters. Big Show would not reveal his own political leanings (outside of bad jokes) but encouraged youth to vote.

Linda McMahon told the *Los Angeles Times*: "We are doing a good thing and we are proud of it. We don't just capitalize on it during election years. This is a real grass-roots effort that keeps going during the years in between." McMahon also spoke of the benefits: "We've gotten the attention of people who did not know our brand before." The LA Times was quick to point out that no one should expect the candidates to get too close to the wrestlers, "with their violent antics and raucous fans."

Gary Davis, VP of WWE's Vice President of Corporate Communications, stated that "Back in 1999, some parents groups were complaining about us . . . this has given us a different kind of profile, a different perspective on our brand. Davis said "We have a very strong eighteen- to thirty-four-year-old audience that watches us week in and out. Why not energize them to do something positive for that community?"

Representative Robert Ney, a Republican from Ohio, attended a Smackdown Your Vote! event in 2004 and "mixed it up" with Kurt Angle. Ney's press secretary said it was beneficial in at least one way: Newspapers that wouldn't normally give much coverage to Ney ran the picture.

Mick Foley and John Bradshaw Layfield engaged in a political debate at the University of Miami as part of Smackdown Your Vote. Each was paired with local students and politicians to debate issues that Bush and John Kerry were expected to debate on the national stage at the same university. Foley was teamed with student, "Terror" Tiffany Yelder and Bradshaw partnered with Alex "The Animal" Acosta.

Foley would represent Kerry while JBL would

represent Bush. Memorable points from Foley included "The Republicans use 9/11 to justify every move they make," While Bradshaw stated that the Democrats considered the tragic event as overblown: "That's like saying FDR and Churchill made too big of a deal out of Pearl Harbor." The Iraq war was also on the forefront. Layfield said "We are greeted as liberators. Fifteen of eighteen provinces are cleared to hold elections." While Foley focused on the President's military service: "Bush has never fought and watched young men die. If he had, maybe he wouldn't be so quick to send young men off to die." Portions of the debate were expected to air on *ABC News Now* and was moderated by ABC's Jake Tapper.

High schools were chosen to participate in mock debates under the Smackdown Your Vote! banner. Miramar High School was one of three Florida locations chosen and the students, Tirmain Sheffield and Antonio Polonco, debated on the same podium used in the actual Presidential debates between 1988 and 2000. Gary Davis said that "We want to foster interest among students in democracy and the election process . . . We want them in on the experience." Mick Foley, Chris Nowinski and Mark Henry were in attendance.

In 2003, Jesse Ventura received an award from the International Wrestling Institute and Museum in Newton,

Iowa. He was awarded the Frank Gotch Award for elevating the status of professional wrestling through his work as a politician. At that time, he said the only political office he was interested in was President.

Trump saw Ventura again when he was interviewed by him at WrestleMania XX, which he attended at Madison Square Garden in 2004. Ventura had been inducted into WWE's Hall of Fame the night before as part of the company's extended WrestleMania weekend festivities. Trump attended with one of his sons, Donald Trump Jr. Trump was greeted with a mild reaction when his name was announced. Trump said, "I was involved with Vince for a long time. He is a great guy. He does an unbelievable job." Ventura (bald, in a bandana) made fun of Trump's hair. Ventura asked if he would receive the support of Trump if Ventura went back into politics and was given assurance of one hundred percent by Trump that he would. Ventura teased that maybe the country needed a wrestler in the White House in 2008 and announcer Jerry "The King" Lawler said that perhaps there should be a billionaire as the next Vice President of the United States, a reference to Vince McMahon. About the time of WrestleMania XX, Ventura was reported to be interested in a White House run in 2008. He planned to run as an independent. He did have concerns that being President would be restrictive of his free spirit nature. His wife had told him that she wouldn't join him in the White House and he had a novel idea; move the White House to Minnesota.

According to the Federal Election Commission database, Linda's political contributions were first listed in 2000 and were relatively modest between 2000 and 2004. It included two contributions to the Connecticut Republican Federal Campaign Committee totaling $6,000 and three contributions to a candidate named Stephanie Hunter Sanchez for a total of $2,000. The fact that the candidate bore the combined name of her daughter and the stage name of her future (and then current) son-in-law had to be purely coincidental. In 2006 and 2007, McMahon donated $10,000 and $5,000, respectively, to the Democratic Congressional Campaign committee.

Chris Nowinski, a Harvard-educated wrestler, and later a concussion safety advocate (as head injuries ended a promising career early), became more involved in the campaigns in later years. In addition to representing the company at political events, Nowinski, now known as a "WWE Political Reporter" hosted a podcast to reflect on how George W. Bush did in his State of the Union Address in 2006. For a company in search of mainstream respect, Nowinski's Ivy League pedigree was an important asset, even if it was often displayed as subtlety as concussion worthy chairshot to the head. Val Venis, a wrestler with a porn actor gimmick, got in on the action with his own political call-in show. He'd later become an outspoken libertarian and marijuana advocate.

Linda McMahon became a Trustee of Sacred Heart University in 2004. Its president, Anthony Cernera, spoke glowingly of McMahon: "Her work as a trustee has been serious, focused and thorough . . . she's got a very sharp mind and can read a business plan and analyze numbers very effectively." McMahon first became involved with the university when invited to speak on work-life balance for women and was later invited to its board. The university, now having featured a speaker series in her namesake and a commons area bearing her name, released a survey on September 20, 2006, in conjunction with Smackdown Your Vote!: "The war in Iraq, national security, the perceived downturn in the economy and the increasingly high cost of education are weighing heavily on the minds of young Americans."

In 2006, Linda McMahon failed to vote in the general election and the Republican primary. She also missed several local elections. McMahon owned up to it when asked by the *Hartford Courant*: "I talk all the time about how important it is for people to vote. And it is. Yet I haven't always been the best example myself. I regret it, I apologize, and I don't make any excuses for it. I think it's important that leaders be willing to step up and own their mistakes when they make them."

Trump's next WrestleMania appearance was his most high profile yet. The financial success and worldwide attention of WrestleMania XXIII is directly attributed to Donald Trump, his on-screen rival Vince McMahon, Jr., and the stipulation for the match. Bonnie Hammer, an executive at USA Network overseeing WWE's shows, was said to have given McMahon the idea of running a storyline with Trump, according to Vince.

Trump's television show The Apprentice had been on the air since 2004. Originally envisioned with a different executive in the decision-making chair every season, it became clear that Trump was the star of the show. The premise of the show quickly changed from a focus on the contestants and challenges to a focus on Donald Trump. His catchphrase, "You're fired!" — which McMahon would claim in storyline that Trump stole from him — swept the nation and became a regular part of water cooler talk the day after an episode aired. Every show featured elements of the Trump brand, such as Trump Tower or the Trump jet.

By 2007, *The Apprentice* had grown stale and its ratings had dropped. Hammer saw a WWE angle as a way to help ratings for both programs. The sixth season of *The Apprentice* drew seven and a half million viewers on average, as compared to around twenty million on average in season one. The season seven renewal for *The Apprentice* was up in the air at NBC, and there was a possibility that the program would not be renewed.

In addition to a potential ratings boost for *The Apprentice*, Trump was convinced to participate in the angle when McMahon offered to make a sizable donation to charity. Donations from both sides were expected to be in excess of four million dollars. Trump did donate all his money to charity, specifically the Donald J. Trump Foundation. Dave Meltzer of the *Wrestling Observer Newsletter* reported that this was the largest payment to a talent in the history of pro wrestling, topping payoffs to Mike Tyson, Dennis Rodman and Floyd Mayweather. The event was expected to draw a crowd of 70,000+ with a projected one million pay-per-view buys at a price of $49.95. Trump was excited about the idea of participating in a record setting show.

Things kicked off quietly in 2007. In a hint of what was to come, Vince McMahon mentioned Donald Trump on *Monday Night Raw* in early January. He said that Trump had stolen his catchphrase ("You're Fired!") and McMahon was going to stop letting people take advantage of him. A stand-in Donald Trump, played by wrestler Ace Steel, appeared for a match versus a fake Rosie O'Donnell, a.k.a. Kiley McLean, who had retired from the ring two years due to nagging knee injuries.

After being recruited by WWE agent Mike Bucci to play the role, Steel acquired a red tie and a suit. Steel considers his brief moment in the national spotlight as a fond memory. He recalled that while he practiced for the match in front of Vince McMahon, McMahon was really enjoying the show and laughing heartily.

In real life, O'Donnell had called Trump a snake oil salesman. Trump responded by calling O'Donnell a real loser and fat. Speaking during WWE's *New Year's Revolution* pay-per-view event, announcer Jonathan Coachman said the feud sounded like something that would happen in wrestling. McMahon agreed and said that they should resolve it the following night on *Monday Night Raw*. In the storyline, McMahon was especially excited about his bottom line: "Think about the publicity, think about the television ratings."

A WWE press release to boost publicity for the event included the following: "WWE will finally let 'Rosie' and 'The Donald' duke it out in the ring on tonight's *Monday Night Raw*. As these dead 'ringers' for both titans are so close to the real people, please consider the below for a fun on-air news bit."

On the show, McMahon announced the combatants to the ring and said that O'Donnell was arriving "in all her lesbionic fury." McMahon described Trump as a personal friend, a billionaire and someone like himself who took pleasure in firing people. The segment was quickly booed by fans. Chants included "this match sucks" and "TNA!" (not an obscene reference to women's private parts but the name of a competing wrestling promotion).

The segment was thought of as an embarrassment by those within WWE (with the possible exception of Vince McMahon). Clips appeared on *Entertainment Tonight*, *Access Hollywood* and *TMZ*. The matchup between the Fake Donald Trump vs. Fake Rosie O'Donnell on January 8 was voted the second worst match of the year by *Observer* subscribers. The only match voted worse was in the TNA promotion, a blindfold match.

Wrestling insider Bryan Alvarez speculated on what was to come in the pages of *Figure 4 Weekly*: "The point is that Vince McMahon's mention of Trump last week and the Trump/Rosie match on Raw is only the beginning of what will end up a program between Vince and the real Donald Trump. Seriously. There were negotiations a few weeks back to start up a program that would culminate at the Royal Rumble, but we're told plans have changed. Trump will appear but not for several more weeks, perhaps at the Rumble or on Raw the night after."

Insiders could not yet imagine the magnitude and money drawing abilities of this wrestling storyline. The Royal Rumble is arguably the second highest profile show on WWE's calendar. It seemed feasible that this storyline could take place live on Monday nights during WWE's flagship television show or perhaps on a major pay-per-view like The Royal Rumble, but the main event of WrestleMania? Highly unlikely.

Within the context of the storyline, Vince claimed that Trump sent him a letter: "Dear Vince, as a lifelong fan of WWE I feel compelled to comment on last week's Rosie O'Donnell-Donald Trump skit. I found the skit poorly produced, inept, lame and quite frankly not up to your standards." McMahon, of course, had to respond to the letter with a letter of his own: "Dear Donald, now that your issue with Rosie is simmering down, it's no surprise that her television ratings are once again in the toilet. And while the Apprentice is going well, it could be doing a whole hell of a lot better. How? By having a very special guest on the Apprentice, a huge star, and that star would be me. By having a very special star on the Apprentice, ratings would soar. Why? Well, because I've been on television for over thirty-five years; wherever I go people tune in to see me. Hell, I single-handedly carried the ratings for *Monday Night Raw*; my presence alone is responsible for USA being the number one network in all of cable. I don't know whether it's my good looks, my charisma, my business acumen, or my Herculean physique, bottom line is people all over the world love me."

The real Trump appeared on screen during fan appreciation night (in tribute to Vince McMahon) during the January 29 edition of *Raw*. Coming the day after the Royal Rumble, it was considered the official start on the road to WrestleMania (sixty-two days away) and what a start it was.

In another hint of what was to come, McMahon made a reference to the broadcast location of the show, Dallas, as he said that cowboy hats were stupid because they mess up your hair and hair is very important to him. Trump appeared via video link just in time to interrupt a segment where McMahon revealed a super-sized cover of himself, at sixty-one, appearing on the cover of *Muscle & Fitness* magazine, a magazine founded by old WBF rival, Joe Weider. The fans did not boo but hardly reacted.

Trump stated that fans know value, at which point thousands of dollar bills were dropped on the audience. "Vince, you claim you tell your audience what they want, what they like, and all of that nonsense. They want value. Who knows more about value than me, Vince?"

McMahon was struggling to keep up with Trump on the screen. Either the segment was recorded or there was a delay in the satellite feed and it made for an awkward and unnatural exchange between the two. The money falling from the ceiling was legitimate bills of various denominations between $10 and $100. Vince was angry that Trump would steal his spotlight and give away his money: "That's my money, *damn it!*" How Trump would have obtained McMahon's money to give it away was not explained.

This early conflict was to allow the water to simmer before it came to a boil to build to WrestleMania. *CNN Showbiz Tonight* covered the rivalry in a segment entitled, "That's Ridiculous." It was also mentioned on ESPN's *Pardon the Interruption*. In 2012, Trump remembered the moment on one of WWE's programs as the time he gave away McMahon's money so that people would like him better.

Trump would not appear on every episode of *Raw* in building up a storyline to culminate at WrestleMania. The next week Trump sent, you guessed it, another letter (I guess two guys in their sixties didn't prefer email): "Dear Vince, I received so many compliments from dropping money on your audience last week that I've decided to up the ante. Next week, I, Donald Trump, will be appearing on *Raw* in person in your very ring, and I have a business proposal that will change your life forever."

McMahon said that he'd also have a proposal for Trump and he'd like to introduce him to a club. McMahon had a running storyline at the time called the "Kiss My Ass Club," where he would actually pull down his pants and performers would have to do as the name implies to his bare bottom on live television. Those "inducted" included son Shane, announcer Jim Ross, and Michael Hickenbottom (no pun intended), known as Shawn Michaels, wrestling main-eventer, locker room troublemaker, and one-time *Playgirl* centerfold.

On the February 12 edition of *Raw*, Trump would travel to the arena in Portland, Oregon. While Vince was making his way to the ring, a sign was held up saying that "Vince Got Trumped." McMahon praised Trump as a television star, a powerful and influential person and until a couple of weeks ago, someone he thought of as a good friend. The announcers clarified that it would be the real Donald Trump in the ring tonight. Jim Ross continued to heap praise on Trump, saying that he had power, influence and a hit show. Trump came down to the aisle accompanied by two WWE "Divas," Torrie Wilson and

Ashley Massaro. Wilson's post WWE career was most notable for being the girlfriend of New York Yankee Alex Rodriguez from 2011–2015. Massaro's relationship with WWE was more fractured as she alleged that the company persuaded her not to report an alleged sexual assault at a military base in Kuwait that resulted when she attended a goodwill mission on behalf of the company. Massaro passed away ten days shy of her fortieth birthday. The first meeting in the ring of McMahon and Trump was met with a technical snafu: Trump did not have a microphone to speak into. After McMahon said Trump was intimidated to come into the ring, he asked the audience to hold on while he got him a microphone. Given McMahon's quick temper, the technician responsible for the microphone trouble likely did not have a good night once McMahon caught up with him backstage. McMahon repeated a previous assertion that Trump stole his catchphrase and that he knew Trump didn't like the Rosie-Trump skit earlier in the year. Trump, never one to miss an opportunity, says that O'Donnell was ugly. The crowd cheered. Trump was fairly restrained, given his ongoing feud with the celebrity. Trump had previously called O'Donnell a loser, a slob, a degenerate, and "Fat Little Rosie" as well as offering condolences to her future in-laws when she got engaged.

In what felt like a quick escalation of the storyline, Trump challenged McMahon to a match; McMahon, before responding to the challenge, already had the headline set: *Battle of the Billionaires.*

"You are a rich guy. I am a richer guy." Trump goaded McMahon further: "I'm taller than you. I'm better looking than you. I think I'm stronger than you, and I am here to challenge you to a match at WrestleMania." Trump was later praised for his ability to ad lib his lines and to manipulate the crowd.

McMahon said regretfully that he couldn't do that as he had a broken pelvis and coccyx (the fans enjoyed the pronunciation of that particular word). McMahon had a counter proposal: Each find a WWE Superstar to act as their representative in the match. Fans booed. Trump twice said he didn't like it. In possibly a first, Trump said he didn't want to put money on the line but suggested each should put their own hair on the line as a stipulation in the match: the loser would get his head shaved. After turning the match down initially, McMahon agreed after some goading by Trump. The match was on. Ross heaped on more praise before the men leave the ring, "Two of the biggest deal makers have made a deal!"

Jim Ross recounts in his second autobiography, *Under the Black Hat*, that Trump was a bit intimidated in one of his first appearances backstage around the talent: "Donald Trump was body conscious, to say the least. He arrived at our TV taping almost as fixated on the guys' bodies as on the women's. Almost. After a few minutes of walking around among the tightest, most ripped, tanned bodies on planet Earth, The Donald was suddenly wearing a large, heavy overcoat, even though he was clearly too hot."

The show was seen by 5.9 million viewers. In comparison, smaller wrestling rival, TNA-Impact Wrestling, did a .59 rating on Spike. When the hair stipulation was repeated in a video at the next night's *Smackdown* tapings, the audience audibly gasped, likely considering the prospect of Trump losing his distinctive and much-debated locks.

4 WRESTLEMANIA XXXIII: BATTLE OF THE BILLIONAIRES

Donald Trump, to a certain extent, represents a great deal of Americana.
Vince McMahon

Trump is in a world he can't understand. This isn't real estate.
Jim Ross, wrestling announcer

Due to WrestleMania XXIII's unfortunate scheduling on April Fool's Day, the company had to make it clear that the stipulations of the match would be honored. "If Trump loses, he shaves his head" said WWE spokesman Gary Davis in an interview with the Associated Press. Trump was aware of whom many of the fans wanted to see lose, telling the *St. Louis Post-Dispatch* "A lot of people want to see [me] shaved. I do get criticized [about my hair], there's no question about it, although I'd never had any problem with it." McMahon said he was looking forward to using dull-bladed scissors and yanking out some of Trump's hair by hand.

Bonnie Hammer may have proposed that Trump participate in WWE programming, but the idea of hair-versus-hair came from the wrestling side. A match stipulation of hair versus hair, with the loser getting shorn, is a familiar sight in the world of professional wrestling. In 1962, a down on his luck George Wagner, better known as wrestling's first television star Gorgeous George, lost his hair to the Destroyer at the Olympic Auditorium for his last big payoff. George died the following year.

Jerry Lawler had used this stipulation many times for increased revenue at the Mid-South Coliseum box office. The records show two consecutive wins over Memphis mainstay Bill "Superstar" Dundee. In the second matchup, the already-shorn Dundee put his wife's hair on the line.

Most notably, Austin Idol defeated Lawler with excessive cheating in 1987. The fans, enraged to see Lawler's hair shorn, rioted. Twenty minutes after the match, the fans were still circling ringside and Idol and accomplice Tommy Rich literally ran through a sea of fans to get back to the locker room.

Hair matches remain popular in Mexico to this day. A Mexican wrestler, who has already lost his mask, can expect a big payday if he agrees to lose his hair in a Mask versus Hair or Hair vs Hair match. However, hair matches were only an occasional stipulation in a WWF/WWE match, most notably used as part of Brutus "The Barber" Beefcake's gimmick

Before the in-ring representatives for McMahon and Trump were finalized, producers and writers of WWE behind the scenes considered several scenarios. These included matching up Shawn Michaels (a popular performer in the mid 1990s, who had missed wrestling's biggest boom period due to an injured back) versus Booker T (a charismatic star from WCW who'd later be inducted to WWE's Hall of Fame the same year as Trump).

Another proposed scenario included Shane McMahon, son of Vince and Linda, against Hulk Hogan. That idea was rejected, and Hogan was then mocked in absentia by McMahon as he threatened Trump with the "brother look," a bald head with hair in the back. Hogan's speeches were notable for using the word "brother" multiple times.

For the Bakersfield, CA edition of *Raw* on February 19, there was a barber shop pole on the set and a barber's chair in the ring. As McMahon made his way to the ring, a fan held up a "Vince Fears Trump" sign. McMahon discussed how he was going to beat up Trump. McMahon, reminding the fans that the show was forty-one days away, demonstrated the sharpest looking cutting implements. To drive home the stipulations of the match, McMahon showed a picture of pop star Britney Spears with her hair and without hair (the poor portrayal of women continues as a running theme in this feud). In a missed attempt at humor, McMahon showed some Photoshopped pictures of Trump with three different hairstyles: a mohawk, a flat top and dreadlocks.

Trump was not in attendance, but McMahon announced his representative for the match: the late Umaga, who had long standing familial ties with WWE as part of the extended Anoa'i family. The family is made up of the Wild Samoans (including Afa, the star of McMahon's steroid trial), the late Yokozuna, and current superstar Roman Reigns, while Peter Maivia and his grandson Dwayne "the Rock" Johnson were both treated as honorary cousins despite having no blood ties. Umaga, who had debuted in 1995, was being promoted with a fresh coat of (face) paint as an unstoppable "Samoan bulldozer."

On the February 26 edition of *Monday Night Raw* from Fresno, California, McMahon expressed some concern as to who Trump would name, noting he tends to one up people, for example: "Someone marries a hot chick, Trump gets divorced and marries a hotter one." Trump did not attend this event either as he was back to participating via satellite on the big screen.

Ending the week-long anticipation, Trump announced that his surrogate in the hair-versus-hair match: Bobby Lashley, the ECW Champion.

Trump, appearing on screen, said Umaga was impressive, but he could go one better. Referring to Umaga as an animal, he said he had a man that could tame the animal, namely Lashley. After the inevitable chaos broke out in the ring, McMahon decided that a guest referee was needed. That referee was eventually named "Stone Cold" Steve Austin.

Lashley had been a US Army service member and amateur wrestler of note. When an injury dashed his 2004 Olympic dreams he joined the world of professional wrestling. Due to his larger-than-life muscular look and athletic background, Lashley was quickly signed to a WWE developmental contract and was assigned to Louisville's Ohio Valley Wrestling school. He was fast-tracked to the big leagues due to a lack of stars at the time and given the low-positioned ECW World title to build his credibility.

Lashley was ecstatic to be selected for the main

event of WrestleMania later, noting "I knew he [Trump] was going to bring a tremendous amount of attention at a point in my career when I could use a boost." Both Lashley and Umaga were up-and-comers at the time and, it was hoped, positioned to benefit from an association with stars of the magnitude of McMahon and Trump.

The ability to stretch out the storyline once the competitors and guest referee was announced became challenging. The March 12 edition of *Monday Night Raw* was in Washington, D.C. Even in their choreographed rivalry, McMahon heaped more praise upon Trump, noting "Trump wrote a bestseller, called *The Art of the Deal* . . . but this is one deal that *he'll regret.*"

When signing the match contract, Trump was accompanied to the ring by two WWE divas. One of those divas, Maria Kanellis, would later participate in *Celebrity Apprentice*. In his syndicated column, journalist Alex Marvez reported that WWE fired her before she appeared on that show as the company didn't take kindly to performers taking on outside projects. Kanellis was fired on *Celebrity Apprentice* by Trump for her use of locker room talk, according to Trump. Kanellis told fellow competitor Curtis Stone, a celebrity chef, "the reason why I said you were so arrogant was because you came in our dressing room and you took a crap and left the stench in the room."

Two years after the recording of his infamous conversation with Billy Bush, Trump said he would not stand for inappropriate discussions.

In their final in-ring confrontation before the big match, McMahon and Trump began referencing unsubstantiated poll results to prove the support their corners had in the match. McMahon claimed "Here you are a show biz mogul and ninety-five percent of celebrities want to see you shave your head. Trump retorted "ninety-five percent of Hollywood celebrities want your head shaved" to which Vince replied "ninety-five percent of this audience are idiots!"

Special referee Austin made his way to the ring. Blessed with the gift of gab, Austin proceeded to talk circles around McMahon and Trump. Perhaps reflecting what much of the audience was thinking, Austin told Trump that he was looking a bit stiff. Trump maintained his ground but did not retort, just raising his chin a bit. The segment ended with the first physical violence between Trump and McMahon: Trump shoved McMahon over a table in the ring and McMahon took a pratfall.

The Battle of the Billionaires in Detroit, Michigan had nearly arrived. There were just a few more press appearances to get through including the March 28, 2007 press conference that took place in Trump Tower in New

York City, the Wednesday before WrestleMania. The Trump logo was placed with equal stature to the WrestleMania XXIII logo on the press conference banner. A barber's pole was in place at the corner of the podium. Donald Trump Jr. and Eric Trump were in attendance to watch the festivities.

As he introduced Trump, announcer Jonathan Coachman called him "the embodiment of the American dream, a best-selling author, a star and producer of *The Apprentice*, and a deal maker who did not have fear. The fans cheered Trump. Trump did not miss the opportunity to promote his commercial building and home to the fans in attendance: "Good looking building, isn't it?"

Trump explained that he had been asked many times to clarify his friendship with McMahon. Trump said that they used to be friends, but now Vince was not a good person and he did not like him. Trump did not appreciate how McMahon treats people. Trump repeated his assertions that he was better than McMahon, taller, richer and maybe even stronger. He later provided questionable facts such that his appearance in Portland drew 30,000 fans in an NBA arena that could hold no more than 20,000, and that WrestleMania would hold more than 100,000 fans in an arena set up for 78,000.

McMahon was likely proud of Trump's hyperbole

here, as McMahon himself, infamous for exaggerating his own live event attendance figures. McMahon reportedly believes statistics shared within the context of his programs are to be thought of as "pure entertainment."

During the segment, McMahon was constantly interrupted by fans yelling "*What?!*" an unfortunate downside of a Steve Austin catchphrase that caught on with the fans in an unexpected way. Austin called Trump and McMahon to the center of the podium for a stare down and photo opportunities. In a surprise, McMahon extended his hand for a handshake. Trump took the bait and was ready to shake. McMahon pulled his hand back and motioned that he is combing his hair. McMahon became more emboldened and began feeling the quality of Trump's suit and swatting his tie around. Trump said something inaudible and slapped McMahon in the face.

Keith Schiller, a long-time Trump security officer (and later White House Security Aide), shoved McMahon hard. Schiller may not have been aware of what exactly was pre-determined and what was not, or perhaps got overexcited, as the force of the push could have injured McMahon in advance of the big event. McMahon quickly left the set looking dejected and holding his face. Trump would tell a reporter backstage that McMahon had no right to put a hand on him, was trying to play around with him, and deserved the big wallop that he gave him.

The slap was covered on ESPN television programs *Pardon the Interruption* and *Around the Horn*. Trump had to be given a fact sheet for interviews so that he could mention the appropriate participants and dates. On the Don Imus radio show, he described Lashley as "Lindsay" and "Lizzy," while identifying him as a "black gentleman, and the strongest man I've ever seen," with zero body fat. When Trump was on CNN with Wolf Blitzer, he cleverly avoided naming either competitor, and would not respond when questioned, as if it were a pre-arranged show or a sports competition. He did say that he hoped his man won. In Trump's appearance on David Letterman, he didn't mention WrestleMania at all.

The souvenir program sold at WrestleMania featured surrogate combatants Umaga and Lashley on the cover, but surprisingly no Trump or McMahon. The program described the night as "WWE's most coveted titles and massive egos are on the line." The program correctly predicted that Trump might become the first person to upstage Mr. (Vince) McMahon at the event and that Trump was proving that no one can "trump Trump"; it also guaranteed that one billionaire would have a shaved head in another attempt to mitigate any doubts.

In the hours leading up to the WrestleMania

match, Trump was featured in a backstage segment on the pay-per-view. While sitting with 2006's Miss USA Tara Conner and complaining about how badly he'd been treated thus far, Trump was greeted by Martin Wright, known as The Boogeyman, an African American man in his 40s with face paint and tribal costume who was most noticeable for drooling worms out of his missing front teeth. Trump looked back at him without a reaction.

In addition to Miss USA, Trump brought Miss Teen USA Katie Blair and Miss Universe Zuleyka Rivera to the event. All three pageant winners sat in the front row, behind the announcers table. In another skit, demonstrating Vince McMahon's long time affinity with potty humor, Trump was shown backstage with McMahon's daughter Stephanie. A baby carriage was also present and supposedly Vince's granddaughter was inside. (Stephanie's first daughter, Aurora Rose Levesque, was born on July 24, 2006.) It was all a set up for a one note joke: Stephanie said that there was a funny smell and that the baby must have taken a "Trump."

The WrestleMania match had finally arrived. Trump made his way to the ring to "For the Love of Money," the theme song of *Celebrity Apprentice* featuring the lyrics, "Money, money, money, money," while money dropped from the ceiling. Trump removed his overcoat to prepare for action later.

McMahon mimed pulling his hair off to show Trump what could happen to him later. Trump acted as a cheerleader to his charge, Lashley, during the match: "C'mon Bobby. C'mon Bobby. Shake it off, Bobby!" Trump had learned Lashley's name.

During the match, Trump goaded McMahon at ringside: "You want some? You want some? Come on up here. Come on up, Vince. You want some? Let's go." Trump had the opportunity to clothesline McMahon to the ground in the match. He went to the ground with McMahon, throwing punches while both were down. When Trump returned to his feet, he smoothed out his tie.

To commentator Jerry Lawler, it sounded like McMahon hit his head so hard on the ground that he should have "been knocked out for a week." McMahon's eye swelled later that evening and had to be covered with makeup for *Monday Night's Raw* program. Lawler, known for his pro wrestling days for throwing a beautiful looking fake punch that did not hurt, may have been on to something. In a practice session the stand-in for McMahon, Armando Alejandro Estrada, the on-screen manager of Umaga, said that Trump was hitting with all his might, as if he was trying to hammer nails into a wall. Estrada ended up with welts on the top of his head. He recounted that he was asked by McMahon about an hour and a half before the match to make sure Trump was ready for the physicality that was going to ensue. Trump wanted to know where McMahon wanted to be punched and Estrada suggested the side of the neck or the top of the head. Following the "practice session," Estrada took ibuprofen to manage the swelling. He kept his signature hat on for a few days, as well.

As Trump became more animated during the match, commentators Lawler and Jim Ross noted his physical exertion: "Do I see sweat on the brow of Donald Trump? That's billionaire perspiration. He probably pays people to wipe his brow."

The actual match itself was overshadowed not only by the McMahon-Trump dynamic outside the ring but by "Stone Cold" Steve Austin as the special referee. Austin, along with the Rock, were credited with the success of the "Attitude Era," the company's late '90s rebranding campaign. Austin fit the time period like a glove, as the cursing, bird-flipping authority-defying and general hellraising caused for Austin's popularity to explode.

Not too far removed from a historically popular run as the biggest star of the company, a star like "Stone Cold" would be hard to contain in just a referee's shirt. It clearly casted a long shadow over two up-and-coming main event talents. Austin was not afraid to get physical in the match, at one point pulling Umaga's hair and at another applying a chokehold.

Over the course of the match, Lashley dove outside the ring, nearly crashing into the barber shop setup. Vince and Linda's son Shane had his turn in the main event spotlight as well. Shane McMahon came in the ring, throwing punches at Lashley. Shane propped a trash can on a dazed Lashley in the corner. Shane went to the opposite corner of the ring and demonstrated his athletic ability, by jumping and driving his legs into his prone rival. As the match devolved into further ridiculousness, Shane removed his shirt and revealed a referee's shirt underneath. Austin recovered from getting knocked down and took out Shane.

Trump couldn't even believe what he is seeing: "What is going on here?!" Jim Ross commented. "Trump is in a world he can't understand. This isn't real estate." Ross was not yet aware how far Trump could extend himself outside of the world of real estate. Shortly after the Trump tackle, Lashley defeated Umaga. Ross stated "The hostile takeover of Donald Trump on Vince McMahon has happened at WrestleMania." Lawler, expressing concern, said "Trump has laid hands on McMahon."

After the match concluded, McMahon held his hair, looking nervous. Normally, only the winner of the match gets his hand raised. In this case, Austin raised not only the hand of Lashley, but Trump as well. Trump waited patiently in the corner while McMahon was brought back to the ring for his comeuppance by Lashley who put McMahon over his shoulder and brought him into the ring. Trump watched and gave Lashley a thumbs-up gesture.

Jim Ross prepared fans for the forthcoming payoff of the match and reminded them why they paid for the show: "Looks like we will have a bald billionaire." To settle McMahon into the barber chair, Austin delivered a "Stone Cold Stunner" to McMahon as Trump cheered the move. Austin then helped Trump to shave McMahon's hair after the match. Trump celebrated with a "Woo!" and clapped.

Trump quickly grabbed an electric razor and asked McMahon how he was doing as he sat in the chair. McMahon screamed as if he was being tortured. Trump used all of the weapons in a barber's arsenal to get the job done: a razor, a clipper and handfuls of shaving cream, with an assist from Lashley. "Bald Headed Blues" played over the stadium microphone. Somehow, McMahon escaped without any significant cuts. Even in a losing effort, McMahon was praised by Ross during the broadcast, "One of the most successful men in business, McMahon in his own creation (WrestleMania), has been humiliated."

Upon the conclusion of the haircut, Austin gave Trump a surprise Stunner after tossing him a beer. (Trump does not drink: his brother Freddy died as a result of alcoholism aged 43.) Jim Ross yelled, "Austin stunned the Donald!"

The Stone Cold Stunner is often set up with a front kick to the gut which induces the opponent to bend over. Austin would then quickly turn his back to the opponent, clamp his bicep around their neck and violently snap them down to the mat; a reverse neckbreaker, in pro wrestling parlance. The Stunner was not practiced in advance of WrestleMania. It looked amateurish in execution—though Trump's hair remained in place—and was arguably the worst stunner seen on WWE television since the now-retired Austin stunned Linda McMahon on *Monday Night Raw* in 2005. It was a risky move for an untrained professional, though, and could possibly result in a severe neck injury if not delivered or taken correctly.

In an interview with *Complex*, Austin detailed how it all became possible. Vince McMahon was enthusiastic about inquiring if Trump would take the move. He introduced Trump to Austin and inquired, "If Steve could hit the Stone Cold Stunner on you?" When Trump wanted to know if it would be a good idea, McMahon told him that it would "blow the roof off the place." Austin explained how the move would work. He may have demonstrated it on another wrestler to give Trump a better understanding. Trump agreed despite his handler vehemently arguing against it.

There was some tension over the weekend between Trump and McMahon and what would take place on the show. As the show drew closer, Trump's anticipation grew and he said that he was ready to have fun. Trump's handler felt that he had nothing to gain and a lot to lose, such as a sustained physical injury, by taking the Stunner. Trump left the event unscathed, physically. "It wasn't a picture-perfect Stunner, but I give Donald Trump a hell of a lot of credit for being a man." Austin gave props to Trump for taking the move and being a stand-up person, though he was more candid when he used an expletive normally reserved to describe excrement in saying how the move looked.

During the WrestleMania broadcast, announcers Ross and Lawler considered the implications of the stunner: "What a lawsuit that will be! I bet that Trump's ex-wives will be doing cartwheels. It is better than alimony!

That's a real hostile takeover!" Journalist Dave Meltzer said that Trump's reaction to the move made Linda McMahon look like a great wrestler in her limited on-screen appearances.

Trump was lavished with praise from WWE talent and backstage producers who participated in the event. Bobby Lashley, Trump's charge for the main event, found him easy to work with. Lashley stated that Trump played right along and Trump was willing to do what WWE wanted to the best of his ability. Lashley feels that Trump received a "bad rap." Lashley feels that Trump has to do some of the things he has done to be a good businessman and leader. Lashley did not see any signs of racism in Trump during their interactions.

Jim Ross felt that Trump was as accommodating as any celebrity the company has utilized in his memory. Ross said that Trump was willing to do things, like take the Stunner and clothesline McMahon, that were not easy for someone of his age, un-athletic body and untrained status. Ross admitted that some of the moves looked ugly in a wrestling context but he admired him for trying. Ross appreciated that Trump complimented him on his announcing skills. Although Trump was accommodating, it was not without hesitation according to Ross: "I had seldom seen a WWE guest who was as nervous about getting physical as Donald was. 'You're going to look after me? You sure now Vince?' Trump asked. "I'll bring you through it Vince replied. "Because I don't want to look like a loser."

Court Bauer, a WWE producer at the time, said that Trump did not have any issues with the things that were being written for him. Bauer went on to say that Trump would even have suggestions for progressing storylines. However, not all remembrances by Bauer were of his easy going nature. Trump would get tired of doing multiple takes and let the production team know that they got what they got and that was it.

Upon Trump's representative winning, the Associated Press announced that "One of the world's most famous fashion 'do's- considered by many to be a fashion don't- remains intact after its owner, Donald Trump, prevailed in Sunday night's 'hair match' at WrestleMania."

Trump and McMahon were not yet ready to give up the spotlight. They appeared together the day afterward on NBC's *Today Show*. Host Ann Curry was photographed rubbing McMahon's bald head outside the studio, while Trump looked on beaming. Another photo showed Matt Lauer and Campbell Brown listening intently to McMahon while Trump watched. McMahon and Trump were also photographed amicably talking together, putting aside their on-screen rivalry publicly. Given the popular morning show airs on NBC, this may have been another coup by Bonnie Hammer of synergy in the NBC Universal family. Trump was ready to give up the on-screen rivalry as he said he liked McMahon again. McMahon vehemently denied that and said that he didn't like him. McMahon was hoping to maintain some sense of friction, in case of a future rematch. Trump said McMahon would probably want a rematch but we'd all have to wait and see. Behind the scenes, McMahon proposed that Trump participate in the following month's pay-per-view but Trump declined.

WrestleMania was a major financial success. It was a complete sell out. WrestleMania earned $31.4 million in revenue and $9.7 million in pre-tax profits. The show was ordered by a record 1,250,000 viewers worldwide of which 825,000 were in North America. In the April 26 2009 edition of the *Wrestling Observer Newsletter*, industry expert Dave Meltzer called the Vince McMahon vs. Donald Trump hair vs. hair feud the most successful short term rivalry ever done in wrestling. In retrospect, Vince McMahon said that shaving his head was the right thing to do. He felt that the public probably thought he would be the one to get his head shaved as Trump's hair was in the public's consciousness regularly, but there was some doubt, which helped to sell the event.

To commemorate the match, you could purchase a few souvenirs featuring Trump. A WrestleMania 23 poster has Trump and McMahon front and center, with the words Hair vs Hair prominently displayed. A similar image is available on the ringside chair that WWE provided for those in the most expensive seats to take home after the event. The picture of Trump appears where one would place his or her posterior if they were to sit in the chair.

The *Monday Night Raw* after WrestleMania is traditionally a time to wrap up any ongoing storylines from WrestleMania and move on with a new season. The 2007 edition took place from Dayton, OH's Nutter Center. On *Raw*, WWE announced a WrestleMania attendance of 80,103. The actual attendance for WrestleMania was 74,687, which did beat the Super Bowl XL attendance figure of 68,206, held in the same building. The paid attendance was 68,500 with $5,380,000 worth of tickets sold. The event simply could not hold over 80,000 fans with a large stage setup. WWE uses some flexibility in counting the numbers by including talent, ticket-takers, and other event staff, a practice not usually employed by other live event acts when announcing numbers. Not said, of course, was that a wrestling show allowed room for more fans than football game and if the NFL had more seats available for the Super Bowl, those likely would have sold as well.

The show opened with a long running gag of how bad McMahon looked bald. Fans who didn't buy WrestleMania were able to receive their glimpse as well when Bobby Lashley removed McMahon's fedora. McMahon, as the majority owner of WWE, demanded that the slate be wiped clean. He wanted the match to be removed from the record books. Unfortunately, a few months later a real tragedy meant McMahon would have to wipe the slate clean and remove one of his wrestlers from the record books.

Although seemingly "in on the act" in WWE, Donald Trump had trouble separating fact from fiction. Just a few months after WrestleMania XXIII, Vince McMahon participated in a storyline where his limousine blew up just after he stepped inside. The closing segment of *Monday Night Raw* played out oddly. McMahon was walking around backstage slowly while maintaining his John Wayne saunter. All of the wrestlers were standing in rows as he walked from one hallway to another. McMahon was told by Jonathan Coachman that he was going the wrong way. He turned around and walked down another hallway to look up at Pat Patterson before exiting the door himself. While walking out the door, he saw two guys passing a joint between themselves and looked back at them quizzically. McMahon continued walking slowly to his limousine and opened the door very carefully. When he closed the door, the limousine exploded. Following the broadcast, Donald Trump called WWE to inquire if McMahon was OK, an incident recounted by Paul Levesque on the *Opie & Anthony Show*.

A WWE press release from June 12, titled "Who Blew Up WWE Chairman Mr. McMahon?," speculated that the saboteur might have been Donald Trump himself: "An official investigation into Monday night's events is currently underway with no one being ruled out as a suspect. Throughout the night, people from Mr. McMahon's past—from Donald Trump to Snoop Dogg to Bob Costas to "Stone Cold" Steve Austin—had less than flattering things to say about WWE Chairman, but would any go so far as to actually blow him up? The question of 'whodunit' as well as the fate of Mr. McMahon, will be on everyone's minds as WWE saga continues on 'Monday Night Raw' on USA."

In an article supporting the storyline on WWE's website, Trump was grouped in with "top media moguls" who'd want to hurt McMahon and hinder WWE's growth. In addition to Trump, those named included McMahon's old rival Ted Turner and Trump's nemesis, comedienne Rosie O'Donnell.

The storyline was dropped a week later due to real death within the company. Tragedy is no stranger to the world of WWE, with so many young wrestler deaths, but this occurrence was especially shocking and heart wrenching. Chris Benoit, a fan favorite known for his intensity and technical prowess, his wife Nancy (a former performer herself known simply as 'Woman') and their son Daniel were reported dead the day of *Monday Night Raw*. That night's show was cancelled, and tributes were given by other wrestlers and classic Benoit matches shown.

As the truth came out that Benoit had murdered his wife and son, then took his own life, McMahon announced that Benoit's name would never be heard on WWE programming again. While his bouts can be seen on the online WWE Network service, he can't be found through the service's search engine.

Revisionist history did not end there. In 2020, WWE Network premiered a *Ruthless Aggression* documentary, a special centered on WWE's in the 2010s. In it, we found this: "In summer 2007, Vince McMahon abruptly cancelled his storyline death, deciding that his newest initiative just could not wait: an expanded Wellness Policy and ban on chair shots to the head. WWE was the talk of the media for months thereafter." Just like in all other corner's of WWE Network, Benoit was scrubbed from history for a more convenient truth. In 2010, Linda McMahon's political rival, Richard Blumenthal, would bring Benoit's father to Hartford to talk about his son during the campaign season.

In an episode filmed in late 2007, Vince McMahon finally had the opportunity to appear as a guest advisor on Trump's *Celebrity Apprentice*. The episode, which aired originally on January 24, 2008, was entitled *A Knight on Broadway*. Each team was tasked with selling tickets to a Broadway show, with the team who sold the most tickets winning. Given McMahon's history of selling tickets to events that could be described as theatrical, it was a natural fit. McMahon was more low-key than usual. He observed both teams' setups in Times Square. McMahon was concerned about the mundane setup of the Impresario team as it did not seem to sell many tickets. In the end, the appearance was largely forgettable.

In 2008, AT&T provided a number that fans could text for more information on registering to vote or in the words of WWE's biggest star, John Cena: "Text WWE to RTVOTE, now!." In conjunction with Cable in the Classroom, WWE provided teachers with short form videos on a number of hot button topics like healthcare, the economy and education. Talent was sent to both the DNC and RNC: Batista joined the Democratic National Convention and Mr. Kennedy and Mickie James represented the promotion at the Republican National Convention.

The URL, vote.WWE.com, is no longer active. The last post on the Facebook page (with 108,000+ likes) was in 2010 and asked "Thanks to all of you in WWE Universe who voted in this year's national elections. What did you think of the results?." That year, some WWE shows had a table dedicated to the campaign.

Acknowledging the voting influence that WWE viewership could have on the election, Barack Obama, Hillary Clinton and John McCain appeared in pre-taped videos on April 22's edition of *Raw* to pitch the fans as to why to vote for each of them in the primaries.

Jerry Lawler, in introducing the candidates, did not suggest any preference for one over the other. In what came across as hokey on the night before the Pennsylvania primary, each candidate name dropped several wrestlers' catchphrases that they had likely never heard before.

Hillary called herself "Hilrod" and McCain said that he was "The Mac." Obama chose to invoke The Rock in asking if the fans "smelled what Barack was cooking?" while McCain said that his words were "the bottom line" (a popular portion of Steve Austin's rhetoric). When WWE would replay the Obama and McCain portions when they emerged as the candidates, Obama would be cheered and McCain booed the majority of the time.

Kevin Horrigan in the *St. Louis Post Dispatch* took major issue with this appearance: "Great: five years into endless war; 4,050 US troops dead; 25,000 wounded; 600,000 with traumatic brain injuries or serious mental issues; the economy in the tank and people being forced out of their homes. And our leader and would-be leaders are goofing for game show viewers and wrestling fans, people who arguably shouldn't be allowed to vote."

Following the actual candidates appearing via video on Monday Night Raw, Hillary Clinton and Barack Obama impersonators engaged in a 'debate' of sorts, full of catch phrases and comedy before the match.- Obama was about to win after delivering The Rock's finishing move, the Rock Bottom, and was about to deliver his patented People's Elbow before Bill Clinton, who was at ringside supporting Hillary, interfered. Umaga then came out to attack both candidates and the match was declared a draw. There was no goofy stand-in for the Republican candidate (McCain).

Linda McMahon was nominated by Governor Jodi Rell for a seat on the 11-member Connecticut State

Board of Education in December, 2008 (it was publicly announced in January, 2009). McMahon first met the Governor when Rell served as a Lieutenant Governor and has contributed to her campaign. Rell issued a statement: "Linda clearly understands the skills and education needed to succeed in business and the type of highly educated and skilled workforce that must be available to ensure that success." In an additional statement from the Governor's office: "If the Governor had any concerns, she wouldn't have forwarded her (McMahon's) name."

There were questions at her confirmation hearing over past steroid abuse allegations and sexual themes that the company had used in storylines. In her confirmation hearings, Representative Janice Giegler, a Republican representative from Danbury made it clear: "We're not putting WWE on the board, we're putting you on the board." One legislator, Representative Shawn T. Johnson, told McMahon that when viewing WWE's website in advance of their meeting that he had to quickly close his office door: "I was afraid someone would think I was viewing pornography on a Capitol computer." McMahon responded to concerns about sexuality in WWE's storyline that its programming has a variety of themes.

McMahon used a credibility association at the hearing that has long been used by pro wrestling promoters: "Did you know Abe Lincoln was a professional wrestler who travelled around in the carnival circuit?" It is well known that Abe Lincoln was an amateur wrestler but the fact he travelled with a carnival may have been a stretch. She offered up her business perspective and trustee experience with Sacred Heart University. McMahon was accompanied by WWE's Vice President of Global Public Affairs, who distributed a pr pamphlet featuring endorsements from Stamford Mayor Dannel Malloy and Secretary of State, Susan Bysiewicz. McMahon was described by the Hartford Courant as having "fled from reporters." She quickly made her way to Governor Rell's office. She was confirmed by a margin of 10-2. In February, McMahon was approved by the Senate 34-1. Senator Joan Hartley, a Democrat in Waterbury, Connecticut, cast the only vote against McMahon. She felt her business skill set would be better utilized on a corporation's board, rather than an education focused one: "I don't doubt her business skills. Quite frankly, I find the sport to be bordering on the barbaric."

McMahon served a little over a year in the role, with her focus quickly turning to a run at the US Senate. McMahon felt that newly issued restrictions on political activities on March 5, 2010, could complicate her political aspirations. Members of the board were now considered "department heads," which limited political solicitations and contributions. McMahon felt that the decision does not preclude one from running for political office but is too restrictive from attending political and fundraising events in order to run successfully.

One aspect of the vetting process for a seat on the board did complicate matters for McMahon: Her answers of "no" to a few questions that could have been "yes," according to Jon Lender of the Hartford Courant. The questions included associations with controversial issues, associations with a person or group that could impugn one's character and any potential embarrassment in one's past. While one could attempt to draw connections between McMahon, WWE and these issues, McMahon stated that they were all known to the public. McMahon was told by the Hartford Courant that they planned to publish a story on this matter and she resigned the next day but claimed one had nothing to do with the other.

5 DONALD TRUMP: OWNER OF RAW

World Wrestling Entertainment announced the sale of its ratings juggernaut, Monday Night Raw, on USA Network to Donald Trump. The terms of the deal were not disclosed.
-USA Network Press Release

On the June 15 2009 edition of *Monday Night Raw* from Charlotte, North Carolina, Vince McMahon announced that he had "sold" Raw to Donald Trump – something that was in fact pure storyline

The announcement was kept a secret, even to those working for WWE. Trump hadn't been seen in WWE for over two years. Within WWE, only Vince McMahon's closest executives knew that Trump would show up. Ric Flair, a mainstream celebrity in North

Carolina, was invited to the show under the impression that he would play a role that had actually been reserved for Trump. This was a red herring to trick fans, wrestling media and even those in the company. The word had gotten out as to Flair being named at least to a storyline role of power: a fan held up a sign that read: "Flair=New GM." With Flair kept in the dark, the reveal of Trump must have been quite the surprise as well. Flair, one of the most popular wrestlers of the last 35 years, has been brought back to television intermittently in subsequent years, at the whim of McMahon.

Trump was not in attendance for the big announcement that he was now the owner; McMahon was instead interacting with a video of Trump. The fans were not exactly impressed and either reacted with groans or didn't react at all to the news. Fans had a difficult time suspending disbelief. McMahon said that Raw would be independently owned and operated. What exactly was McMahon selling in selling Raw? This was not made clear. Trump did make it clear that he would not be in attendance every week but promised to do things that had "never been done before, never been seen before."

Similar to the satellite interactions of McMahon-Trump in 2007, the feed appeared mistimed and Trump was talking before McMahon had a chance to respond.

Trump, looking very orange (likely due to an aggressive spray tan), said that he was now the sole owner of Raw and he would make sure the fans were shown appreciation. McMahon denied that he hadn't treated the fans well. Trump said that McMahon should give back (which Trump repeated for emphasis).

Trump announced that the following week's program would air commercial-free, thanks to his generosity. McMahon thought Trump had lost his mind. Trump reminded Vince of the time he shaved his head. McMahon would be in attendance to say goodbye. Before Trump was done for the evening, he ordered a pay-per-view worthy matchup between two top competitors next week: Triple H versus Randy Orton (a third-generation wrestler), in a Last Man Standing match. Giving away a match that could draw money on pay-per-view, along with the commercial-free episode, were both genuine expenses for the promotion: USA paid WWE $550,000 per episode and would want to be compensated for the loss of commercial revenue. This would not be the end of "giving away money" in the Trump storyline.

It was speculated that Trump's return was designed to help build further on synergy with the NBC/Universal related networks. Donald Trump was still actively involved in The Apprentice series and WWE was part of the family, with their programming airing on USA and other NBC/Universal properties. Due to the success of WrestleMania 23's "Battle of the Billionaires'," it was thought at the time that this could lead to a rematch down the line at 2010's WrestleMania XXVI. It was only natural that a long-awaited feud would continue at some point due to the revenue potential. Most newsworthy was that USA Network sent out a press release regarding the sale, entitled "Trump buys Raw—first show commercial free":

World Wrestling Entertainment announced the sale of its ratings juggernaut, Monday Night Raw, on USA Network to Donald Trump. The terms of the deal were not disclosed.

Commenting on the deal, WWE Chairman Vince McMahon stated, "This was an offer I couldn't refuse."

"The Monday Night Raw franchise has been one of the top cable franchises since its launch 17 years ago," said Donald Trump. "I'm going to do things on the show that have never been done or seen before. As my first act as owner, I am doing something unprecedented. I am giving back to the people who have been loyal all these years. For the first time in more than 838 episodes of Raw, next week's show will be live and commercial-free.

Mr. Trump will be making his first live appearance as the new owner of the Raw franchise this Monday. The episode will run commercial-free on USA Network at 9 PM ET/8 PM CT."

"Donald Trump is one of the most entertaining personalities with *one of the sharpest business minds of our time. He's always had the Midas touch, which will only add to the level of excitement for the loyal fans of WWE Monday Night Raw," said Chris McCumber, EVP Marketing, Digital and Brand Strategy for USA Network."*

The storyline "sale" was considered an actual financial transaction by many business outlets. For example, on June 16 2009, StreetInsider.com ran the headline, "Donald Trump Buys World Wrestling Entertainment's (WWE) *Monday Night Raw*." The story listed that terms of the deal were not disclosed and, as per the press release, said it was an offer that McMahon could not refuse. The article was filed on the site in the "Corporate News, Mergers & Acquisitions" category.

Once the news organizations realized it was a storyline, many pulled their reports. Some business analysts wondered how a publicly traded company could provide information in this confusing manner. USA had to issue an apology: "USA Network and WWE issued a press release on June 16 that referred to *Monday Night Raw*'s storyline of a 'sale' of WWE's *Raw* to Donald Trump. We intended the release to be promotional for that ongoing story arc on the series. There is no such actual 'sale.' We apologize for any inconvenience."

The stock price dipped as a result of the confusion

related to the sale, at one point being down seven percent. Dave Meltzer of the *Wrestling Observer Newsletter* reported that the perception on Wall Street was that only Vince McMahon can run a pro wrestling company. Any other change in management would lead to a drop in value for the company.

The USA Network lost credibility with the sale announcement to the media, who may otherwise have given favorable press to WWE and/or a USA Network program. Outlets were reluctant to be caught with egg on their faces by promoting a press release for the June 22 program. Chris McCumber, the Executive Vice President of Marketing, Digital and Brand Strategy quoted in the press release, would survive the blunder. He would work his way up to co-President and ultimately President at USA Network.

The hope was that the commercial-free episode would lead to attention and an increase in ratings that would carry over to subsequent weeks. A press conference was held on the morning of the show. It was a starkly different look from the press conference held at Trump Tower in New York City to support WrestleMania XXIII. This conference was held at the Austin Straubel International Airport in Wisconsin. In the *Green Bay Press-Gazette*, Kendra Meinert wrote that "There are Mondays, and then there are Mondays when the Donald is in town. Guess which one is more fun?." In a post tarmac interview, Trump told Meinert that in reference to the fans: "They like Trump. They like Trump."

McMahon said that tonight he would give his farewell address. He seemed more reserved than usual, likely because the plans were already in place to reverse course on Trump as an "owner" and by the end of the night, there would not be much to hype.

Trump's hair was blowing around in the open air space. One of the women that accompanied Trump to the podium was Maria Kanellis. A fan yelled out, "We love you, Maria!" Trump reaffirmed that Maria was loved (a large picture of her is also visible on the ring truck behind the press conference podium).

In an incident from that day, shared by Eve Torres on President's Day in 2020, it may not have been Kanellis that caught Trump's eye.

Prior to the press conference, Trump took a photo with six of WWE's "Divas." Torres claimed that Trump had forcefully grabbed her.

Torres wrote on her Instagram account: "I have taken pictures with thousands of men at military bases, at WWE events, and signings, and very few have grabbed me and pulled me in as forcefully as he did without knowing me. Of course, at the time I believed it was my job to be eye candy in a photo for this supposed billionaire and play along. It is actually hard for me to see that photo because it reminds me of my beliefs about my worth at the time." Generally, Jim Ross recalled that "backstage, Trump's eyes were wandering, and because of WWE's new policy of hiring Playboy-type models for the women's division, there were plenty of places for The Donald's eyes to wander."

To draw cheers and curry favor with the fans, Trump told them that he had long been a Green Bay Packers fan. Trump said that when he decided to make the investment, the first thing he thought of was to put the green back in Green Bay. McMahon appreciated the line and was smiling. Trump told the fans that ticket money would be refunded to fans that night, and this was the first time something like this has happened, not only in wrestling, but all of sports. Trump speculated that 22,000 fans could be in attendance; in fact the Resch Center arena has a seating capacity of 10,200 (further reduced to about 8,000 with the Monday Night Raw setup featuring a Jumbotron and entrance ramp).

McMahon, attempting to jump back into character, was ready to take back the podium. Trump put his arm around McMahon to say how much money he is giving back. McMahon had little to say and opened the floor to the media. There did not appear to be much media in attendance and fans yelled out questions or just shouted. One question was asked as to why this event was held in Green Bay. Trump stated that it was a great sports town while McMahon remained silent due to the unclear ownership and decision making for storyline purposes. Of course, the event in Green Bay had been scheduled several months in advance. It was not the most impressive media showing by WWE and it was difficult to provide the perception of an exciting event, even in short clips shown that evening. A photo shows McMahon and Trump laughing and chatting affably off-camera during the event.

KFC was the main sponsor of the advertisement-free show, including having a bucket of chicken prominently placed at the announcers table. The Wall Street Journal was also featured on the program but it is highly unlikely that it was paid for. Despite WWE regularly championing the organization's work with The Special Olympics, Festus, a large character playing a not so subtle role of a person with developmental disabilities, was shown leaving a bathroom with the *WSJ*, seemingly having read it while doing his business, and then handing it to McMahon as a sight gag.

The show opening song for Monday Night Raw

usually features the wrestlers. In an impressive detail, Donald Trump took up a significant portion of the show-opening song, along with his properties and holdings (it was too bad that it could only be used for one week). A Trump logo was now affixed to the Raw logo, most resembling a gold bar. Announcer Michael Cole welcomed fans to the Donald Trump era. The fans were ready this time for Trump, as there were several signs shown on screen including, "Got Trump?," Trump Trump$ McMahon," "Trump>McMahon," "Raw Got Trumped," and most curiously given WWE's high praise for Trump's business acumen, "Trump finally invested in something good!"

Trump announced from the ring that all of the fans in attendance would get their money back, a return of $230,000 to paying fans (or as Trump stated, $245,000). Naturally, this led to cheers. He said that he is the only one that would do that for fans. Signs were posted in the arena as to how fans could receive the refund of their money. Trump emphasized that the fans should wait until the show is over to inquire about a refund, a line driven by a fear of many fans leaving their seats to get a refund while the show was ongoing. The return of the money did not sit well with some of the 10 percent of WWE's workforce that had been cut within the last couple of months as a cost-cutting move.

Trump reminded fans that he provided a top-notch match for the night, better than McMahon would have given them. Trump was portrayed as getting the only high-quality limousine in Green Bay, Wisconsin while McMahon's broke down. Trump took over McMahon's office, leading to frustration for McMahon. Donald Trump Jr. was in the audience, behind the announcer's table, enjoying the show. In an odd scene given WWE's current anti-bullying campaigns, Trump met a cross-dressing wrestler, Ms. WrestleMania, played by WWE regular comedic figure, Anthony Carelli, known as Santino Marella. Trump could contain his disgust at seeing a man in drag, and fired him, noting "I'm doing the same thing to you that I did to Ms. California," The Ms. California referenced, Carrie Prejean, was under fire for her stance on opposing same-sex marriage and because barely clad photos of her had surfaced publicly. She was able to weather these storms but Trump fired her around this time period for not "fulfilling her duties." Perhaps WWE's writers remembered the Ms. WrestleMania storyline fondly, as Marella returned to the company after several years in the 2020 Royal Rumble. His role? "Santina" Marella, a contestant in the women's Royal Rumble, a sight gag as Marella was dressed in a top with silver stars, a mini skirt and wig.

The storyline of ownership became more convoluted but was nearing its conclusion as the night wore on. Trump returned to the ring and stated that he did not believe in General Managers. The fans "whooo'd" in return. This reference to Flair was probably not on Trump's radar. Instead of a GM, Trump would bring in more celebrities and high-profile people every week. The fans were not impressed.

Trump began talking about WrestleMania XXVI but McMahon's music interrupted him. After experiencing one night of on-screen frustration (and one week of disappointing fan interest), the McMahon character was ready to wave the white flag. McMahon felt that he was being setup by Trump, in that Trump would force McMahon to financially support Raw and McMahon would eventually go bankrupt by letting fans in for free and not having any commercial television revenue. With Trump serving as the owner in the storyline, this argument did not exactly make sense but rash decisions had to be made and some sort of reason given. Vince McMahon would have to buy back the show.

In order to demonstrate his sharp business acumen in the storyline, Trump did not agree to a sale until McMahon offered double the purchase price. Trump was not willing to take a lowball offer as he said that since he bought Raw, he could do whatever he wants. The fans were quiet when Trump shook McMahon's hand on the deal. McMahon invoked Trump's best-selling book once again, *The Art of the Deal*, in saying he knew Trump has to negotiate but it wasn't fair.

Once both parties had agreed on a price, the McMahon character felt emboldened again and threatened Trump. He told him that if he ever saw him again (or any affiliated Trump logos), he would knock him on his billionaire butt. McMahon then told Trump, "You're fired!," a phrase that they both made famous on different programs. The storyline was left open ended as Trump slapped McMahon in a final act of defiance. The fans, despite being given up on by Trump in pursuit of a solid return on his investment, chanted his name in unison. Trump slapped McMahon. This would make a total of three physical attacks by Trump on McMahon, without any retaliation. The announcers were quick to point out that, "We've just seen the *Art of the Deal*!"

The June 22 show was a rating success with a 4.53 Nielsen rating and 6.8 million viewers. It was the highest rated show since March of 2004. Viewership increased to 7.8 million viewers by hour two.

Variety credited Trump for the ratings success,

and did not mention that the episode being commercial free might have helped with the overall rating. Despite the rating success, the decision was made before the second episode featuring Trump to end his involvement as the owner of Raw. The original storyline was scheduled for much longer than one week but McMahon was not impressed with the reaction that it received from the fans. The storyline as originally planned might have carried the company for six months (or even into WrestleMania XXVI, as Trump briefly alluded to).

According to *Figure 4 Weekly*'s June 23, 2009 issue, a former writer made note of the following: "You can't capture the same magic twice. When we used Trump last time he was at the height of his public feud with Rosie. Now he's very cold." Despite the storyline non-starter, the company was considering ways to get Trump back involved as soon as possible. He would not be a player with the company again until 2013, being provided status as a celebrity inductee in WWE's Hall of Fame.

All of the attention on Trump had more immediate effects within the company. The upcoming pay-per-view, The Great American Bash, was not properly promoted due to a lack of airtime and was the third least purchased show in several years. With Trump leaving, WWE's need for celebrity spotlight continued. A series of "guest hosts" (as suggested by Trump, despite no longer being in power) were lined up for several weeks. They included Jimmy Fallon, Ashton Kutcher, Rachel Ray and Danny DeVito.

The Donald J. Trump Foundation received a further $1,000,000 for his participation in this two-week storyline. The Smoking Gun website later examined the foundation's finances and reported that the total of $5,000,000 paid by WWE was more than Trump himself had donated to the foundation over a 20-year period ($3,700,000). The WWE stated that it was Vince McMahon personally (and not WWE) who donated this money.

In addition to direct contributions to Trump's foundation at the time, the McMahon's may have provided Trump a favor in a real estate transaction. In October 2009, the McMahons purchased a condo, a 3,900 square foot duplex penthouse, at Trump Parc Towers in Stamford for $4.1 million dollars. About a million dollars over its market value at the time. The purchase was a high profile buy for a property that was seeking attention and sales. At the time of the purchase, only two of the six penthouses had been sold with the McMahon's purchasing the largest unit (only between 25-30 units in the whole building had been sold at that point). The McMahons lived in Greenwich and had no plans to move to Stamford (despite it being the location of WWE's corporate offices). At one point, the McMahon's were 51 days late in paying taxes on their property. The McMahon's owned 7 properties at the time of the purchase. Martin Nirschel, a Sotheby's Real Estate Broker said to the Greenwich Time, "In a weird kind of way, (Vince McMahon) is buying into the town because Trump is the apotheosis of the redevelopment down here. This is really the centerpiece, and I think in a way, it's a statement." Nirschel also said, "Who better, really?" By 2017, the property value was down to 1.9 million. Perhaps another in a long line of business misses outside of professional wrestling for the McMahon's or a good investment in staying in Trump's good graces.

On September 16 2009, Linda McMahon, the Chief Executive Officer of WWE, announced that she was resigning from the company after announcing her candidacy to run for the United States Senate. She had been disengaging from her responsibilities in the year prior to explore a potential run. The Los Angeles Times in covering the news wrote that "maybe The Rock and Triple H will serve as campaign managers." Vince McMahon assumed his wife's title of CEO as well as remaining chairman of WWE. McMahon told the Associated Press that she never does anything halfhearted and is one hundred percent serious. McMahon said that she can't sit on the sidelines anymore, presumably in reference to political office and not her overall visibility in comparison to her husband.

The WWE was only about six or seven years removed from its raunchiest content and McMahon had to make a clear distinction to the public: "The product of WWE is currently very separate from the issues that are facing this country . . . I hope that the focus in this campaign will be on the serious nature of the issues that are facing this country." McMahon's WWE ties would be hard for the public to forget as comparisons were quickly made to Jesse Ventura's run for Minnesota Governor. Ventura said that he tried to warn McMahon before she ran of the pitfalls such as any potential skeletons in her closet. Ventura had no plans to support McMahon as he never supports candidates from traditional parties.

Some saw her experience in WWE as getting her ready for the rough world of Capitol Hill but she was quick to dismiss it: "The product of WWE isn't going to prepare me for D.C. any more than 'The Terminator' prepared Arnold Schwartzeneger to run for Governor of California."

By 2009 and in the years that followed, checks of

over $10,000 and often over $25,000 were commonplace from Linda McMahon to Republican centric causes. This included the National Republican Senatorial Committee ($30,400), Boehner for Speaker ($25,000) and regular contributions to the Connecticut Republican SCC. As McMahon had given to Democratic candidates as well, The Next Right labelled her as a "Liberal Wrestling Promoter."

Linda's political knowledge had also been enhanced through her connection to Lowell Weicker, Jr. not only a former Connecticut Governor but a Senator. Weicker said of Linda: "The intelligence factor is very much a part of Linda, she's a very decent lady." In 2010, he said, "I wouldn't sit on its board of directors unless I was proud of the company and I am . . . Whether you're good or bad in the product, you sell, people vote with their feet and they're playing to packed houses all over the United States."

Linda McMahon ran for Senate in Connecticut in 2010 and 2012. Both times she spent about $50,000,000 on the campaign, most of which was her own wealth. She was proud to tell reporters that she wasn't obliged to any major donors or other influencers as she wasn't using their money. She ran a campaign in 2010 that a businessperson was needed due to her success in turning WWE into a publicly traded company: "You know about living on budgets and making a payroll." By the 2012 campaign, her strategy shifted away from emphasizing a WWE background.

In 2010, Mike Lupica called it the "dumbest, silliest time in the history of politics, it figured that pro wrestling would run a candidate for the US Senate." Despite not being employed by WWE at the time, Hulk Hogan was firmly in the other camp: "I think she's going to win. She's brilliant. She's a very gracious, very smart lady, and her intent and her agenda has always been to help the community and be plugged in and be involved. Inside or outside the wrestling that the McMahons have created, Linda McMahon is a great person."

At that time, it was the most that any candidate had spent of their own money in a bid to win a seat at a federal level. In Donald Trump's successful presidential election bid, he spent $66,100,000, so McMahon outspent Trump when combining her two campaigns. Trump did state that he spent $100,000,000 but official filings showed that was simply not the case.

Margaret Carlson of the *Pittsburgh Post Gazette* utilized McMahon's candidacy in 2010 as the opportunity to take a dim view of the Republican Party as a whole: "It's hard to imagine the hatred voters must harbor toward

Washington to make Ms. McMahon a viable candidate. For the Republican Party, which stokes that hatred, no imagination is needed." Carlson felt that following McMahon's primary victory that the GOP is now moving from "the year of the outsider to the year of outside the bounds of normal behavior." Dante Ramos in the Boston Sunday Globe was more positive, at least of Linda as a person: "She also turns out to be a confident, media-savvy campaigner whose converted her vulnerabilities into selling points." Ramos wrote that she is clearly more comfortable in politics than in an on-screen wrestling role.

Linda and Vince McMahon appeared at Sacred Heart University fundraising event that also had potential Democratic opponent Richard Blumenthal in attendance on April 21, 2010. Vince was reported as getting up, introducing himself to the audience and directing his attention to Blumenthal "My name is Vince McMahon and my wife is the one who is going to beat you this fall." The two were reported as shaking hands later but Vince telling him that Linda was going to "whoop" him in the election. Blumenthal laughed (on the outside, at least).

While Smackdown Your Vote! was still active, the McMahon campaign had a voter registration idea of its own. At the University of Connecticut, students conducting registration would receive an extra five dollars for each person that registered as a Republican. Av Harris of the Connecticut Secretary of State's office said that "It's a practice that the Justice Department has frowned upon." Anthony Esposito, President of the Registrars of Voters Association of Connecticut felt it was unethical. Once the plan received publicity, it was cancelled. Ed Patru, her campaign's Communications Director, said "I'll say that it's important to Linda that everything this campaign does be above board and legal."

As late as September 2010, the Richard Blumenthal campaign did not comment on recent wrestling deaths of WWE performers that included Luna Vachon and Lance Cade. As the campaign got closer to its conclusion, Blumenthal's campaign began to use it as an issue. Mindy Myers of the Blumenthal campaign issued the following statement "The death of these wrestlers is clearly a tragedy. As the people of Connecticut examine Linda McMahon's record as CEO of WWE, undoubtedly there are questions regarding her role and the health and safety of her wrestlers that she needs to answer."

The company initiated a Stand Up for WWE campaign, as a direct result of senatorial race, according to Vince McMahon in the first YouTube video. The purpose of the campaign was to rally WWE fans to reach out via social media and defend WWE against elites who looked down their noses at WWE, the media and "government officials." A series of videos aired featuring long-time WWE employees as well as third generation wrestlers emphasizing how the company was a family. A sub-section of its website would post rebuttals to unfavorable media coverage.

Republican conservative talking head Ann Coulter described the election season in 2010 for Republicans as a "roll of the dice" in supporting McMahon's bid for election: "Let's run a professional wrestling "impresario" for the US Senate . . . hey you never know!" Coulter was not impressed by this line of thinking. She felt that Connecticut's educated populace was going to have to "hold its nose" and elect Blumenthal so as not to support someone from the world of wrestling. She felt that Republicans received a "gift" by the news that Blumenthal had not been forthright in his description of his service in Vietnam and it was being wasted by someone from "professional friggin wrestling."

Despite Lowell Weicker's connection to McMahon, he endorsed another candidate in 2010. He did provide her some advice, however: "I told her this is going to be a rough haul, but she still wanted to go ahead and do it. Linda's a grown-up girl . . . she knows exactly what she got into. It ain't beanbags, it's a tough business."

The Democratic party was prepared to use McMahon's past with WWE against her. As reported in the *Asbury Park Press*, a spokesperson stated: "Today, the party of Bob Dole, Jack Kemp and Dick Lugar nominated a candidate who kicks men in the crotch, thinks of scenes of necrophilia as 'entertainment' and runs an operation where women are forced to bark like dogs."

The man kicked in the crotch was Jim Ross, who had a long history of being humiliated on-camera on the October 10, 2005 edition of *Monday Night Raw*. In this scene, the McMahon's (Vince, Linda and Stephanie) discussed how to maintain power over employees. Linda said, "The only way to garner respect from people isn't by yelling and screaming. It's by taking action. So, J.R., on behalf of the entire McMahon family . . . you're fired." Linda then kicked Ross where it hurts. The kick looked slow and unconvincing but seemed to hit the target. Ross wrote in his book that he wasn't wearing a protective cup. Ross reports that Linda apologized to him in advance of the angle backstage and she was upset at what would occur.

To be fair, there is no evidence that Linda McMahon found the necrophilia angle entertaining. Vince McMahon felt that people were unfairly attacking his business to discredit Linda's candidacy. He thought the necrophilia and female barking storylines were taken out of context. After all, a soap opera would not look so great if you only observed its juiciest moments without the storylines to build it up. McMahon did tell the AP that the company had "made some mistakes" and moved away from shock tv a couple of years prior.

New Jersey Governor Chris Christie hit the campaign trail in support of his fellows Republicans in 2010 including Linda McMahon. His support of 18 candidates would help his visibility if he were to decide to run for President one day. More of the candidates he supported won than lost, with McMahon ending up on the loser column.

Gail Kim, an underutilized female wrestler in WWE at the time (when the company was not big on that sort of thing), wanted to clarify the misconception that WWE and Linda's campaign's for senate were separate. She tweeted that "I find it ironic that some wrestling fans say don't mix wrestling and politics which I believe I don't. You should however know that WWE did mix the two when Linda ran for senate. They literally had a room set up for a video campaign for talent to speak about how great WWE was."

While Vince McMahon publicly stayed away from the campaign, just prior to the election in 2010, he announced that he planned to give away WWE merchandise at select polling locations and that fans should feel free to wear a WWE t-shirt. Upon being informed of strict rules that require no campaigning within 75 feet of a polling location, he planned to give away the merchandise within the acceptable distance. While originally ruled that WWE merchandise could not be worn on election day, Secretary of State Susan Bysiewicz said that voters would be allowed to wear WWE merchandise into the polling booths.

On Saturday, October 30, 2010, WWE held a Fan Appreciation Day in Hartford's XL Center. The 15,000 seat arena was set up for 11,000 and sold out. While the company regularly toured with two troupes at the time, *Raw* and *Smackdown* (consistent with its television brands), this was a combined Supershow, designed to increase interest- including an appearance by HHH, defeating Alberto Del Rio and John Cena defending his world title against Kane. The event was booked only a month in advance and featured ticket prices cheaper than usual, between $10-20 and total gate receipts of $140,000. The WWE wanted to thank the fans of Connecticut for their support "amid the harsh examination of the sport that has accompanied former CEO Linda McMahon's campaign for the US Senate," according to the Hartford Courant. A fan in attendance, Jeffrey Kokiel, held up a "Linda for US Senate" banner from his floor seat.

Vince McMahon even made a rare appearance for a non-televised show. Speaking from the center of the ring, he said "Some people may think I was going to talk about politics today. Nothing could be further from the truth. I do encourage you to vote this Tuesday and while you're voting, feel free to wear a WWE t-shirt." He claimed he had been the subject of lies by politicians and "subject of distortion, equivocation by some members of the media" during the campaign for US Senate.

Linda McMahon's campaign had confirmed her plans to attend the show but she was not there. Her campaign said her schedule was not as flexible as planned as she campaigned in five cities that day. The *Hartford Courant* conducted interviews with a random sampling of fans in attendance and found that she received widespread support. Shannon Thurston said, "They're attacking her family business, which is not really fair. She's not going after Blumenthal's family." Bob Jacobson, a Connecticut resident for 27 years, said he did not know much about Blumenthal but would be voting for McMahon: "I definitely think it's wrong they take wrestling in a negative light. There's a lot of good they do, like charity work."

Just a few days later, on Tuesday November 2, the

company returned to the state for a Smackdown taping in Bridgeport, a heavily Democratic enclave. Federal authorities issued a rebuke to the company that it was coordinating communications with Linda's campaign. Vince McMahon was defiant: "World Wrestling Entertainment will not be bullied or intimidated by whining allegations intended to censor our freedom of speech." The show went on as scheduled.

While WWE avoided advocating anything overtly political at the show, there were vans in front of the arena pushing various Republican candidates, including Linda McMahon. Once inside the arena, there was only one "Linda for Senate" banner visible. Vince McMahon spoke from the ring about voting. He got a big cheer when he told people to wear their WWE T-shirts to the polls, but he only encouraged people to vote without indicating who to vote for.

McMahon's initial campaign was dogged by former wrestling champion, Billy Graham. His body broken down from steroid abuse and physical damage in the wrestling ring, he was furious about having no pension or other levels of support. Graham said that McMahon "May look like a Sunday School teacher . . . Linda McMahon's hands are as bloody as her husband's because she is aware of every move in the ring." Graham attributed some changes in WWE product from the Attitude Era to benefit McMahon's campaign: no more "blading" (intentionally cutting oneself with a razor blade to bleed in the course of a match) as well as no more matches like "Bra & Panties" featuring former Playboy or Hawaiian Tropic models. Graham planned to create a t-shirt featuring a razorblade dripping with blood taped to her finger (the technique for the aforementioned blading) and the words "Linda McMahon is a scam and is made out of spam." No word on if these t-shirts were ever made but it is hard to imagine the product being a popular seller. Graham was only about a year outside of a contract that kept him on WWE's payroll when speaking with the *Hartford Courant* and his support or critique of the company has waxed and waned over the years.

In an ESPN poll conducted around the election season, pro wrestling fans were found to skew as being 60 percent more likely to be Democrats. Additionally, pro wrestling fans were 30 percent less likely to vote as compared to the average person's of the same age group.

In a post mortem on the election, the *Hartford Courant* ascribed McMahon's loss not only to her WWE past but partly for her inability to take a clear stance on Social Security and Medicare related issues.

In April 2011, Lowell Weicker Jr. left WWE's

Board of Directors. He said it was a mutual decision and not connected to not endorsing McMahon during her Senate race. Several other members of the Board resigned during the same time period.

In 2012, McMahon said she was inspired to join the race after looking at the face of her grandchildren. McMahon received several endorsements by former state Republican chairpersons, whose support was expected to help bolster her pool of volunteers across the state for the primary. Chris Healy, Chris DePino, George Gallo, Dick Foley, Herb Shephardson and Bill Hamzy were some of the best-known GOP names in Connecticut. To build support that year, McMahon visited a number of town committees to learn how she could support Republican municipal elections. McMahon formally announced her candidacy at Coil Pro Machinery, to push her brand as a job creator, small business protector and entrepreneur. In the first Republican debate, one opponent Kie Westby, stated that jobs where wrestlers use steroids and women walk around in bikinis are not real jobs. McMahon hoped to shift the focus away from her WWE past and receive more support from women.

Another primary opponent, Christopher Shays accused McMahon of not only being involved in a business that denigrates women, something he described as softcore pornography, but also those with disabilities. He also accused McMahon of providing free tickets to WrestleMania to influence John Slater, the Bridgeport Republican Town Chairperson. A charge McMahon and Slater denied. McMahon said she was proud of the business and jobs that she had created.

There was pressure for McMahon to release her tax returns. On July 21, 2012, she sort of complied. Her opponents had demanded she release her 2011 returns but she released those from 2010. Her spokesperson said that the documents for 2011 just were not ready yet but said that 2011 would look similar to 2010. Filing jointly, Vince and Linda McMahon earned $30.6 million in adjusted gross income, with most of it from investments. They paid $4.7 million in federal taxes and $2.1 million in state taxes. The majority of charitable giving went through their foundation, the Vince and Linda McMahon Family Foundation. Among donations East Carolina University (their alma mater) received $1.6 million. The law firm of Jerry McDevitt, a lawyer with a long history with WWE, had prepared their taxes.

Chris Christie would return to support McMahon in 2012. Christie said that her opponent, Chris Murphy, "might as well be Nancy Pelosi's butler." His one liners, such as "Ms. Pelosi, can I get you a cup of tea?" drew laughs in all three stops: Stamford, Waterbury and Glastonbury. There were hundreds of supporters at each stop, including 400 in Waterbury. Christie was treated like a rock star, according to the *Hartford Courant*. Attendees held up pieces of paper for his autograph and recorded his speech with cell phones. Christie lauded her business acumen and ability to work across party lines in rebuilding the economy. Christie went on to say, "This is a woman who is doing this because she sees the perilous path we're on, she knows the right way to fix our country and you cannot hand this job over to just another career politician who is going to continue the failed course. You've got to send Linda McMahon to the United States Senate." Bill Clinton would be in town a few days later to support Murphy. Senator John McCain also came to town to support McMahon. On October 1, 2012, he spoke with veterans in Danbury and then spoke in an afternoon rally at McMahon's Norwalk field office.

McMahon's campaign was hoping for split ticket support. One advertisement with an African American woman stated: "I'm voting for President Obama, and I'm voting for Linda McMahon. It's my right." One advertisement featured an African American woman who was wearing a clerical collar and identified as a Reverend. Ronald Wislocki, a Tax Manager from Waterbury did not understand: "If you're going to vote for Obama, I don't know why you'd vote for Linda. It just doesn't seem like a complementary vote." Opponent Murphy found the strategy odd as well: "This is one of the strangest political ads I have ever seen because we know that Linda McMahon is going to oppose President Obama on everything that he stands for." Murphy continues, "I mean, there is almost nothing Linda McMahon agrees with President Obama on, which makes this ad absolutely deceitful."

At the same time the McMahon campaign was publicly supporting Obama, Linda and Vince donated $10,000 to a non-profit organization called Americans for Job Security. The organization spent a total of $15,000,000 denouncing Obama during election season. The dark money group did not disclose its donor list until years later.

One of McMahon's ads was named as one of the five worst political ads by the Honolulu Star Advertiser. In the ad, Murphy is attacked for raking in one million dollars. What was not said was that the amount was earned over six years, as opposed to an annual salary. What the people found laughable was the attack on earnings when compared to McMahon's stock holdings with WWE. Overall, Gary L. Rose, author of *No Holds Barred: The 2012 Connecticut Senate Race*, found her ads as upbeat and appealing and was an overall different message from the 2010 campaign. The 2012 message focused on telling a human story as McMahon focused on her North Carolina roots, her young motherhood, past bankruptcy and entrepreneurship. One area McMahon was trying to improve upon was her support amongst women.

Christopher LaCivita, McMahon's Senior Campaign Consultant said that the campaign team had realized early that the impression of McMahon from 2010 was not who she really was. People wrongly believed that she was "born with a silver spoon in her mouth." Two blonde women in one advertisement said that McMahon understood their concerns and her policies would help the people of the state. This compared with 2010 advertisements where two women riding in an SUV came off insincere in its tone when addressing support for the candidate.

Murphy's attack ads focused on McMahon's WWE past as well as her wealth: "As CEO of World Wrestling Entertainment, Linda McMahon had a plan: Shift profits overseas to avoid US taxes; Deny employees healthcare and disability to increase her profit. Now McMahon has another plan: Tax cuts for the wealthy. Including a $7 million tax cut . . . for herself. McMahon's plan for the middle class? Cuts to Medicare and education.

Linda McMahon: Always for her. Never for us." Ads also focused on her cuts to health benefits for employees and layoffs to WWE workers.

Lowell Weicker, Jr. emerged in support of Murphy and more critical this time of McMahon: "He's given a lot of public service, whereas in the case of McMahon, it's been self-service and no public service with the exception of a couple of meetings of the State Board of Education." Weicker went on to say: "It's the ultimate corruption that says you don't have to earn the senator's job and it's out there on the table for the highest bidder." Weicker did say that his support of Murphy has nothing to do with WWE.

The Journal Inquirer's Managing Editor, Chris Powell, wrote two scathing columns that year on McMahon that included that her "practical qualifications for office did not extend beyond her fantastic wealth, and that wealth derived from the business of violence, pornography, and general raunch." The WWE sent a letter to the company that it was engaging in libel. The Journal Inquirer filed a federal election complaint against WWE, accusing the company of illegally abetting her campaign. The complaint was filed with the Federal Election Committee.

WWE's Senior Vice President denied the

allegations: "WWE is not attempting to prevent the media from exercising First Amendment Rights. In fact, WWE itself makes a living exercising those very same rights . . . However, that does not give anyone the right to hide behind the First Amendment to recklessly disregard the facts and state that WWE is in 'the business of pornography.' WWE considers this to have been written as a statement of fact and not opinion by Mr. Powell and the Journal Inquirer: "First Amendment rights should not be confused with blatant disregard for the truth. It is ruthless and in some cases unlawful to disparage a company and its seven hundred employees with damaging misrepresentations. WWE is not and has never been in the business of pornography. Hopefully this will set the record straight once and for all."

Rhetoric heated up between Murphy and McMahon in debates. In reference to the seat being vied for with the retirement of Joseph Lieberman, McMahon stated: "You thought this campaign was going to be a coronation . . . and now you're in a serious race against a serious woman and you are desperate."

The third debate in New London's Garden Theater was most notable for the raucous nature of the audience. Outside of the theater, unionized defense workers for General Dynamic blasted Murphy's name from a flatbed truck, while across the street, a group of young people chanted "Linda! Linda!" while holding a cardboard cutout of Murphy and waving blue McMahon signs. Meanwhile inside, despite being asked by the moderator not to do so, the audiences jeered, booed and applauded candidates at various times. Matt Sledge of the *Huffington Post* described the debate as "a tense carnival stage show." Mary O'Leary of the New Haven Register wrote that the event was closer to a wrestling show. During Murphy's closing arguments, one attendee decided to heckle him. Murphy took a moment to compose himself but placed the blame on his opponent's shoulders: "Quite a crowd of supporters you have here, Mrs. McMahon."

Linda McMahon had spent so much on local television advertisements in the Connecticut market in 2012 that Jim Shea pondered what life would be like "AL (After Linda)." He joked that her presence on television made her seem like a member of the family, as he put it, a cross between an old aunt who gets angry when she drinks and a kindly grandmother. Later in the same column, Shea ran an unrelated story in which he called Donald Trump the "undisputed clown prince of moguls" for offering $5 million dollars to Obama's favorite charity if he only released his college transcripts.

Ann Coulter eviscerated political consultants who advised McMahon to run: "I salute anyone who runs for office as a Republican, but Linda McMahon in Connecticut and John Raese in West Virginia were lied to by campaign consultants who told them they have a chance to win."

McMahon's excessive spending of her own wealth was still being mocked in the *Hartford Courant* in May of 2015. The term "McMahon's Law" was coined for the first time. In the paper, Colin McEnroe termed it as the tipping point in which you spend so much money on your own behalf that people begin to hate you. The *New York Times* reported that McMahon's free spending did benefit her in one way: it took her out of the shadow of the wrestling empire that had been more associated with her husband and helped her to create a political brand in the state. McMahon was often tethered by WWE's past, such as its knack for crass, dated storylines, including Trish Stratus, future WWE Hall of Famer, barking like a dog at Vince's feet. Workers at WWE spent time to remove video links and other references to racier material during McMahon's time at the company, which included WWE's Attitude Era. As she emphasized her role as a job creator, such clips reminded voters of her role in WWE and that didn't prove to be a positive. Only 40 percent of voters felt that

McMahon had high ethical standards.

McMahon took the opportunity to comment on the 2012 presidential race with a fairly liberal outlook on comments made by Mitt Romney: "I disagree with Governor Romney's insinuation that 47 percent of Americans believe they are victims who must depend on government for their care. I know that the vast majority of those who rely on government are not in that situation because they want to be . . . "

While in the midst of her runs for Senate, Linda McMahon donated $5 million dollars over five years to Sacred Heart University to fund capital projects. The new student commons building bore McMahon's name. The 46,000 square foot building would cost $22 million dollars and include a 250-seat student dining area, a private dining area and lounge spaces.

Although Linda McMahon had stepped down from her WWE role, she still held stock in the company. When the news broke that WWE was requesting state assistance to hire more workers, McMahon's campaign was tied into the story. They had planned to hire two hundred workers for what ultimately became WWE Network, a streaming platform, with some limited television distribution outside of the US. The company was hoping to benefit from Governor Dannel Malloy's

Next Five program, which provides millions of dollars for company expansions. When WWE applied, it was compared to Linda McMahon's website where she had campaigned to end "corporate welfare," in which she opposed industries supported by politicians.

While McMahon would once again lose in 2012, it did not appear to have anything to do with ties to WWE according to polling data. In a Quinnipiac Poll released on August 28, 2012, 47 percent said her affiliation to WWE made "no difference" when selecting a candidate, while 21 percent were "more likely" to support her because of it and 30 percent were "less likely." According to Gary Rose, Murphy's win can be attributed to a number of factors including Murphy being able to draft on Obama's political momentum, a larger Democratic political base in the state, a strong get-out-the-vote push the day of the election and changing demographics in the state. Rose concluded that there was little Linda McMahon could have done to change her fate in the 2012 election season.

The *Washington Post* reported that final checks given to campaign staffers bounced. Kate Duffy, McMahon's Deputy Communications Director, said that checks were in the mail but new checks could be issued as well.

When Linda McMahon ran for a senate seat in the

state of Connecticut, Donald Trump donated $5,000 towards her 2012 campaign. The acceptance of that donation was slammed by one-time rival Chris Murphy's campaign team in an email to supporters at the time: "That's right, the man who led the charge to see President Obama's birth certificate, report cards, and test scores has set his sites on Connecticut's Senate seat." In August and September of 2016, McMahon donated $6,500,000 to a super PAC, Rebuilding America Now, which supported Donald Trump during his successful presidential campaign run. In any estimation, a wonderful return on the Donald's investment.

6 HALL OF FAME

WWE is the best . . . I love those guys, that's my family.
Donald Trump

Politics is boring. Wrestling is the better entertainment value.
Kerwin Jacobs

Speculation was building in 2011 about the chances of a variety of potential presidential candidates in 2012. *Reuters* reported in April that Trump led in some Republican polls, but experts did not expect a reality show President. Rich Lowry of *King Features* wrote: "Lets' see . . . the business background of Ross Perot, the outsider combativeness of Jesse Ventura and the marketing skills of P.T. Barnum." An editorial in the *Journal and Courier* of Lafayette, IN, entitled "Trump's GOP": Glitz, opulence and power, included: "The idea of The Donald making a bid for the White House seems more plausible as a plot for a reality tv show or maybe a sitcom. But then, who would ever have predicted professional wrestler Jesse Ventura being elected as Minnseota's Governor?"

On July 23, 2012, the USA Network and WWE celebrated the thousandth episode of *Raw*, appropriately titled WWE Raw 1000. The event took place in the Scotttrade Center in St. Louis, Missouri. To hype the event, special moments in the history of Raw were played regularly on programs aired in the weeks leading up to the event. On its 999th episode, Trump provided a brief interview recalling his favorite moments. Although he had not appeared on the episode, Trump said his favorite show was the Raw after WrestleMania XXIII. Trump enjoyed viewing the aftermath of his victory over McMahon. He was happy to see McMahon's shaven head and black eye. He described the best part of the program as watching Vince squirm and said he loved embarrassing McMahon.

Donald Trump was set to be announced for WWE's Hall of Fame on the February 18, 2013 edition of *Raw*. It appears this was delayed for business reasons: the revenues for the DVD release of the event had not yet been sorted out. Instead, on the February 25, 2013 edition of *Monday Night Raw*, Trump was officially announced as an inductee. As with other inductees already announced in the previous week, the announcement was made in the form of a three-minute vignette.

The video opened with a view of a boardroom and a man turned around in a chair, with the distinctive hair that could only be "the Donald's." A narrator with a voice normally reserved for a movie boomed, "Today, one man has become synonymous with success." Trump then turned around and stated "That would be me."

The song most associated with Trump on *The Apprentice* and in his two most recent wrestling appearances played: "For the Love of Money." The narrator resumed: "Business mogul, best-selling author [all of the book covers were shown], reality television star [shots of Trump on *The Apprentice*: 'You're Fired. You're Fired'] . . . his outspoken personality and business acumen has made him one of the most powerful men in the world."

Michael Cole, a WWE announcer, stated "Donald Trump has been one of the biggest supporters of WWE since the 1980s." Cole served as a political and war correspondent in the 1990s, a fact that WWE would bring up often to build credibility for the company. The video then linked the rise of Trump in the 1980s to the rise of WWE and WrestleMania. As the video concluded, Jerry Lawler could be heard saying "Wow! Congratulations to Mr. Donald Trump!" Lawler seemed particularly enthusiastic for any announcements regarding Trump.

According to Dave Meltzer of the *Wrestling Observer Newsletter*, Trump is more deserving than most for being inducted in the celebrity wing of WWE Hall of Fame. Along with celebrities like Cyndi Lauper, Mike Tyson and Mr. T, Trump was instrumental in the success of a WrestleMania, as well as helping to increase ratings at various points. The attention given to the participation in wrestling of Tyson, T and Lauper was important in providing a mainstream spark to usher in long success periods for the company.

Nearly any celebrity that has some minor involvement with the company has had some consideration for the celebrity wing. The justification for many celebrities is fairly loose. Pete Rose appeared briefly at three WrestleManias, including once in a chicken suit. Drew Carey participated momentarily in a Royal Rumble. Snoop Dogg accompanied his cousin, Sasha Banks, to the ring for a match, guest hosted a couple of *Raw* episodes and emcee'd something called a "BunnyMania Lumberjill" match.

Trump could hardly contain his excitement on Twitter the night before his Hall of Fame induction. He asked his followers to tell him which was cooler, his induction into the WWE Hall of Fame or his star on the Hollywood Walk of Fame. Replies were not unanimous: among several snarky replies that he wasn't worthy of either and some WWE Hall of Fame support, Christine DiStefano replied, "The 'Coolest' is that which you've yet to achieve."

The Hall of Fame souvenir program, an oversized magazine with the WrestleMania matchlist on the back, featured brief profiles on each Hall of Fame inductee. Trump was described as a "billion-dollar business mogul," "longtime friend of sports entertainment," "undeniable powerhouse of personality" and a "key figure in WWE since 1988." The description listed WWE as being proud to have Trump as an honoree due to his proven ability to be a ruthless contender who "will stop at nothing" to knock people over who get in his way in a wrestling ring or in business.

Thef induction ceremony took place in a sold-out Madison Square Garden, the night before WrestleMania. According to the *Wrestling Observer*, WrestleMania weekend, including the highest profile WWE Hall of Fame event in its history, resulted in the highest number of traveling fans attending events in the company's history. Trump's book *Great Again: How to Fix Our Crippled America* claimed that 25,000 people attended the event, a figure far above MSG's true capacity.

Who would be the one to induct Donald Trump? Vince McMahon, of course. It was rumored that Trump insisted on it, but it is likely that McMahon was happy to oblige.

The opening segment of the show included clips of the inductees in various important moments and memorable matches. Trump's section showed him in a casual backstage photograph with McMahon as well as a photo of Trump shaving McMahon's hair at WrestleMania XXIII. The crowd booed him heartily at any mention of his name, well before he took the podium. The booing started early as they booed his inductor, Vince McMahon, and they even booed the man that introduced his inductor, Jerry Lawler. Lawler was proud to reveal that he held a picture he took with Trump in such high regard that it was his Facebook profile picture. Lawler called Trump an icon in business, television and hair.

McMahon didn't receive only boos however. There was a "Thank you, Vince" chant, seemingly for being the man behind WWE and bringing years of entertainment to the fans in attendance. The booing picked up as soon as McMahon spoke about Trump. He called him a WrestleMania institution (counting the next day's festivities, he had attended six out of the twenty-nine shows to date). McMahon said that after WrestleMania V, a relationship was formed between them and Trump was ringside in Los Angeles for WrestleMania VII.

McMahon noted that "When you think about it, second only to me, Donald might very well be a great President of the United States." Fans chanted "Yes!" when McMahon inquired if the fans thought he (McMahon) would make a better president.

McMahon asked fans to wait to boo until Trump actually came out for his speech. The fans started yelling "No! No! No!" McMahon did not seem shaken as he said that Trump knew exactly what he was getting into. McMahon compared himself to Trump, saying that he and Trump both followed in their father's footsteps and some say they had massive egos; McMahon said he didn't see it, in a tongue-in-cheek comment. McMahon said Trump was known for his personal appearance and hair (which then appeared on the big screen). Referencing their "Battle of the Billionaires" clash, McMahon said it was only natural that their egos and hair would clash. He claimed that Donald won because he cheated and McMahon's guy lost. McMahon concluded with, "Ladies and gentlemen, my friend . . . *Donald Trump*."

With genuine in-ring greats being inducted, fans were understandably upset. The night's inductees included Bruno Sammartino, Bob Backlund and Mick Foley. Sammartino held the title on two separate occasions for a number of years and is remembered as a beloved figure in the company's history, especially to the Italian community. Backlund, while not remembered as fondly, was a serviceable champion for many years during the late 1970s and early 1980s. Foley, a more contemporary wrestler, was known for being a champion but more so for sacrificing his body for the delight of fans, such as when he fell off a structure known as a Hell in a Cell in a match with the Undertaker. Foley had to retire early due to injuries sustained in the ring.

After several hours, by the time of Trump's induction the fans were restless to see Sammartino. An introductory video termed Trump as an entrepreneur, visionary and entertainer and now celebrity inductee in the class of 2013. Fans were likely tired of the company trying to tell them what to think when it came to Trump.

One wrestler that Trump had observed at previous WrestleManias also took issue with his induction: Brutus "The Barber" Beefcake. Beefcake acknowledged that Trump had some contributions to the business but was more of a fan, who sat at ringside. Beefcake felt that the Hall of Fame should be for the wrestlers like himself, who had over 35 years' experience in the business. It was likely especially irritating to Beefcake that Trump's wrestling performance is most closely tied to administering a haircut, a regular part of Beefcake's routine. Beefcake received his own induction into the Hall of Fame in 2019.

Donald Trump entered once again to the lyrics "Money, money, money, money." Before he started speaking, fans chanted "You suck!" Trump began by noting that "Vince and I have had an amazing relationship for many years" and that it all began with WrestleMania IV in Atlantic City, NJ. Trump knew to invoke the name of Andre the Giant to gain some cheers when recounting a story about meeting him during WrestleMania IV. The fans cheered, albeit briefly—the Giant actually passed away in 1993.

Trump talked about his parents and how his father Fred felt that seeing his son attending WrestleMania was one of the greatest things he had ever witnessed. Fans booed. Trump went on to discuss how he invited McMahon and the WWF back the next year for WrestleMania V. An audible chant of "*BO-RING!*" came from the audience, not unlike the booing that occurs during a match when one wrestler has another wrestler in a rest hold for an inordinate amount of time, or par for the course in modern-day WWE.

Trump was happy to take credit for drawing the highest pay-per-view numbers for the company. That was true at the time of the show, though was now an outdated claim. A dream match-up of the Rock against John Cena at WrestleMania XXVIII in 2012 had since narrowly edged out WrestleMania 23 by a margin of 1.217 million purchases to 1.2 million purchases. Donald stretched the truth when claiming that he also drew the biggest TV rating ever as well, though he did draw strong ratings. Trump could not resist stretching the truth outside of wrestling as well: he spoke about having the highest rated show on all of television, *The Apprentice*, when in fact that show peaked below the top five of all programming.

Trump introduced two of his children during the speech: "I have to introduce some really great people—my son Eric, my daughter and television star, Ivanka." Eric was booed, while Ivanka was cheered. Trump asked the audience if she did a great job on The Apprentice. The fans agreed with a hearty, "*Yes! Yes!*" Trump was happy at his daughter's reception, responding "Finally, they like somebody!" Her appearance may have played a part in her popularity with the fans. Trump also said that he is married to a great woman, Melania, which earned mild cheers. The fans then chanted "You still suck! You still suck!" The booing for Donald was so loud that he wasn't able to complete his whole speech; a fan was clearly heard shouting "Better wrap it up, B!" at one point.

Inspired partly by the fans' treatment of Donald Trump, ticket holders at the following year's Hall of Fame ceremony received an e-mail from the arena requesting: "Please show the proper respect to WWE Superstars and Hall of Fame inductees when they are on stage speaking. There will be no inappropriate behavior, cat calls or chants of any kind tolerated at all. Violation of this policy will result in immediate ejection from the Smoothie King Center without warning."

Trump said that getting inducted into WWE Hall of Fame was the greatest honor of his life and that he still loved everyone. This was not before he listed previous accolades, such as having a star on the Hollywood Walk of Fame. In a backstage interview following the speech, Trump said it felt great and Vince was an amazing man who he enjoyed laughing and kidding with. He felt a powerful energy that always came with McMahon's company.

The biggest news to come out of the speech was another potential showdown in some form with McMahon. Trump challenged McMahon to a fight and stated that he would kick his ass. Trump said that he knew that he would get the same enthusiasm and love from the fans when that showdown occurred as he has on this night. In a backstage interview, McMahon, not usually one to back off from a fight, didn't seem as enthusiastic to reignite another on-screen rivalry with Trump. McMahon said that he was already sixty-seven, so they'd have to see. Trump tweeted early in the morning following the Hall of Fame Ceremony: "Sorry losers and haters, but I LOVED the great energy in Madison Square Garden during my speech. The WWE thought it was incredible—it was!" In a move that seemed a bit more polished than his tweet, Trump posted a video early the next week, thanking WWE and saying he had a great weekend and it was something special. Before the video concluded, he asked the fans to follow him on Twitter.

Television viewership for the Hall of Fame ceremony would not—and could not—be touted as the biggest or the best by WWE or Trump. In fact, the ratings were a big disappointment as just over 1.6 million viewers tuned in. The program aired in primetime three days later, on a Tuesday, and was below the USA Network ratings average. The previous year's ceremony had earned a million more viewers.

Trump was also introduced in a special ceremony

at WrestleMania XXIX. Along with the other Hall of Fame inductees, he stood upon a large entrance ramp while his name was announced. He played second fiddle as he was introduced before Bruno Sammartino. Boos weren't as audible this time around, but he didn't receive a tremendous ovation, either. Trump later stayed to watch the show.

Matches on the show included the Undertaker defeating CM Punk to continue the winning streak that started at WrestleMania VII, Triple H defeating Brock Lesnar, and John Cena defeating the Rock (in a match billed as "Greatness vs. Redemption" in a rematch of the previous year's main event, which had been tagged as "Once in a Lifetime").

According to Wayne Keown, known as Zeb Colter, Trump's favorite part of the show was Colter's appearance. At the time, Colter was a semi-retired professional wrestler and manager. His career was given new life in the form of "The Real Americans." The faction, led by Colter, was playing off anti-immigrant sentiment among some Americans, with a unique nod to the Tea Party. Colter, a wily veteran and at times a backstage power player, knew how to manipulate a crowd. He had played on nationalistic zeal in Puerto Rico to draw the fans ire and greater ticket sales revenue. The group would conduct backstage interviews and come to the ring with a Don't Tread On Me flag.

Paul Joseph Watson of *InfoWars*, a conservative outlet, felt that the Real American characters were demonizing the Tea Party. Watson felt that this was part of an overall cultural push to divide people and portray groups like The Tea Party, conservatives and libertarians as extremists and radicals.

Colter accompanied Jack Swagger, a tall blond wrestler with a strong wrestling pedigree, for his World Championship matchup against José Rodriguez, known as Alberto Del Rio. The promotion for the matchup was not subtle, playing up a "real American" against a Mexican born wrestler, with deep familial roots in Lucha Libre. Colter's pre-match speech was largely the same as those he had been spouting for months but may have been the first time Trump was exposed to the angle. Colter said that he and Swagger were the real Americans. Colter had the chance to walk the dirty streets of New York and it was not the New York that was usually described but instead was filthy. He felt that New York was no longer worth what it was acquired for as it was a breeding ground for criminals, illegals and people sneaking over the border. He didn't enjoy hearing Spanish, Italian (with emphasis on the "I"), Chinese or "something called Yiddish." He said that the fans were too gutless to do anything about it. He promised that Swagger would reclaim the title that they deserved. Although Colter was playing a villain role, the fans enjoyed the Pavlovian response and chanted along as he finished his speech with the catchphrase "We the People." Despite Colter's rant, Del Rio defeated Swagger in under eleven minutes.

Colter said that Trump went to find him backstage later in the evening. Trump reportedly walked up to Colter, who was with Donald Jr., Eric and Ivanka, and told him how much he enjoyed his speech. Trump yelled "Fantastic!" repeatedly. Perhaps Trump considered the speech in a literal sense, instead of a spoof on hate speech and the Tea Party; Colter is sure that Trump stole his "gimmick."

Just a year prior, the debate on immigration was at the forefront of a smaller wrestling promotion. Lucha Libre USA, a company marketing to the Hispanic community in areas like Arizona and Houston, was utilizing "RJ Brewer" as a heel, the storyline son of Arizona Governor, Jan Brewer. Brewer had taken a hardline stance against immigration. SB1070, signed by the Governor in 2010, required immigrants in Arizona to carry immigration papers and for police, while conducting general business, to inquire regarding immigration status if there is reason for suspicion. The power of good would be defended by Blue Demon, Jr., whose father is legendary in Mexican wrestling circles. The programming appeared briefly on MTV2 and some Spanish language channels.

The day after WrestleMania XXIX, Trump went on Fox News to discuss what he learned about North Korea from Dennis Rodman, whom he'd seen backstage the night before. Rodman, ex-*Celebrity Apprentice 2* participant, had traveled to North Korea many times and built a relationship with leader Kim Jong Un.

Linda McMahon kept her hand in the political scene in the years that followed her defeats. Just nine months after her 2012 loss, the *Hartford Courant* described McMahon as entering her "third act" in politics, as a major benefactor to Connecticut Republicans and advisor to its chairperson, Jerry Labrioli Jr. In the story, Dr. Gary L. Rose, Professor and Chairman of the Department of Government and Politics at Sacred Heart University said "Linda is definitely going to be a player within the Republican party. She's tasted politics and, even though things didn't break her way, she's interested in having a voice."

In 2013, Linda McMahon took a position on the International Advisory Council for APCO Worldwide, a Washington, D.C.-based public relations firm. In 2014,

McMahon announced the formation of Womens' Leadership Live (WLL). The organization sponsored events featuring women speakers and panel discussions regarding promoting business opportunities.

Vince McMahon and Donald Trump would have one more high-profile public exchange before Trump jumped head-on into the world of politics. In the summer of 2014, the ALS Ice Bucket Challenge was sweeping the world of social media. To raise awareness and funds to combat the disease, friends and associates were challenging each other to dump a bucket of cold water on their heads, film it and challenge more friends.

On August 14, WWE posted a video of McMahon in WWE corporate weight room. In a video with over two and a half million views, McMahon accepted the challenge from his son in-law, Triple H. Before dumping water on his own head, McMahon challenged "Billionaire" Trump as he said it would make for a great visualization.

In a YouTube video posted on August 28, 2014, Trump accepted McMahon's challenge (as well as those of Mike Tyson and Homer Simpson). In a video viewed nearly ten million times, Trump managed to one-up McMahon in presentation. The video took place on the roof of Trump Tower, where Miss Universe and Miss USA poured Trump Water into the ice bucket. Trump said that he had been called out by everybody, including McMahon. Similar to the Battle of The Billionaires, the intrigue was whether Trump's hair would be shown not to be real. Before the beauty pageant winners poured the water on his hair, Trump challenged Obama and sons Donald Jr. and Eric. Upon getting wet, Trump's hair hung down like a puppy that's been in the rain too long. Similar to McMahon, Trump remained still while getting drenched.

Although described as "media shy" by *Roll Call* following her election loss, McMahon remained in conversation with Republicans not only around the state of Connecticut but around the country. She continued to invest her money in a variety of Republican causes including a combined $154,800 to the National Republican Committee and the National Republican Senatorial Committee. She also co-hosted a variety of events, including a fundraiser for Chris Christie's Leadership Matters for America PAC. She supported a variety of Republicans that were close to her northeastern base as well as female candidates. As far away as Arizona, McMahon was listed as one of the top seven donors during the 2014 election cycle: her $249,000 in contributions to the Republican Governors Association Arizona PAC, supporting Governor Doug Ducy, landed her between noted national power players Michael Bloomberg and

Sheldon Adelson in the state. Closer to her home, *The Boston Globe* listed Linda and Vince McMahon as donating a combined $2,400,000, the second biggest donors in New England during the 2014 cycle. McMahon's generosity to her party of choice was not without its accolades. In April of 2014, McMahon received the highest honors from the Connecticut Republican Party at the 36 Annual Prescott Awards Dinner at the Stamford Hilton. Jeb Bush was the featured speaker at the event. Bush received much criticism that week from conservatives as he described illegal immigration as an "act of love," undertaken by people hoping to provide for their families.

In addition to her financial contributions, McMahon contributed a series of op-ed pieces, that were published in both local media and newspapers in a variety of states. Her focus was on developing leadership in women. She leaned on her middle school basketball career to extrapolate life lessons.

The articles kept McMahon visible and further distanced her from pro wrestling and two historically expensive failed runs for political office. A 2013 piece in the *Hartford Courant* published on January 26, titled "Focus on Enabling Growth, Small Business" not only hinted at a passion for potentially supporting business owners that will serve her well later, but gave insight into her thinking and perspective at the time: "What if we sought to shift the national conversation from our disagreements to the shared beliefs that unite us as Americans?."

McMahon also had concerns about too much oversight into business: "No one disputes government's essential role to help those in need and to provide for the common defense. There is a legitimate question, however, as to when more government becomes too much government."

7 DONALD AND LINDA GO TO WASHINGTON

Politics is dirtier than pro wrestling.
Jesse Ventura

There are three things you can argue about until you are blue in the face: politics, religion and wrestling.
"Classie" Freddie Blassie

"*He's not helping, certainly, to put women in the best light."*
Linda McMahon

When Donald Trump officially entered the presidential race, WWE posted a message on its Facebook page in June of 2015: "That's right, WWE Universe! We may end up with a WWE HALL OF FAMER for president . . . " 21,000 people hit "like."

On a campaign stop at Crosby High School in

Waterbury, Connecticut, Trump was photographed holding up a picture of himself from WrestleMania XXIII. In the photo, he is about to give Vince McMahon a haircut while Austin held McMahon in the barber's chair. When Donald Trump emerged as a candidate for presidency, there was a groundswell of support from fans for removing him from the Hall of Fame based on comments that came out about minority groups. Ultimately, he was not removed.

Linda McMahon spoke out against Trump's treatment of women early in the 2016 campaign season: "He's not helping, certainly, to put women in the best light,' she said. "Maybe he regrets [his words]. Maybe he doesn't. I realize he punches hard when he punches back, but that's just over the top." Additionally, she called Trump's comments "deplorable" and "objectionable." When Trump emerged as the Republican candidate and stood a chance to win the election, although slim according to regular polling results at the time, Linda McMahon emerged as a stronger supporter, although she admitted that Trump was not her first choice to be President of the United States. When asked on CNN in April of 2016 who she supported, she said that there were considerations, she was not ready to commit, and "yeah, you know . . . " A non-answer as classified by the CNN interviewer. McMahon was giving generously to another Presidential hopeful who has spent his time supporting her, Chris Christie. She donated $250,000 to America Leads, a super PAC supporting Christie's campaign.

McMahon said she found Trump capable of being the Commander in Chief and that he would hire the right advisers. She said she knew him for many years and he was a good man. McMahon later justified Trump's actions by saying that he has been acting as "the vessel" that is demonstrating the dissatisfaction and anger in the country at the time. She described Trump as loyal to the end. Linda was not concerned about Trump's comments about Hillary Clinton, for example that if Clinton was a man, she wouldn't get 5 percent of the vote. McMahon supported how Trump planned to remove chaos, create order, bring jobs and put America first. Linda wasn't concerned about his lack of a specific plan as she said that would come later. She concluded he had great respect for women and hires women, such as hiring his daughter Ivanka, to run one of his companies (revealing about Ivanka's business strategy is a quote from her book, *The Trump Card: Playing to Win in Work & Life*: "Perception is more important than reality. If someone perceives something to be true, it is more important than if it is in fact true").

Officially, WWE avoided any partisan mention of

the 2016 election on television, the web and social media. Vince McMahon would not comment on Trump's presidential candidacy and was said to have issued a gag order directly to his employees, likely for fear of a negative public reaction from segments of his audience due to the divisiveness of the election. The WWE has fans all over the country and the world. Partisan support of one candidate could have hurt their fan interest with supporters of the other candidate; it could also upset business partners who'd prefer WWE stay out of politics.

Several media outlets reached out to current (and former) performers and employees regarding Trump's previous performances and appearances with the company. Word was that former performers called WWE to inquire if they could speak on the record about their feelings on Trump and/or prior interactions with him at wrestling events. Why would a former performer for WWE be beholden to the approval of the company? Every good wrestler knows that another run with WWE is just a phone call away and it is best to stay in the good graces of the McMahons.

Current WWE star Seth Rollins denied any company suppression placed on discussing Trump. Rollins said that it has never been brought up to him publicly or privately by anyone in the company and the guys who want to make political statements do, and those who don't want to, don't. In fact, in October 2019, Rollins was still discussing Trump. At the Fandemic Tour convention Q-and-A, he named Trump in response to which non-wrestler he'd like to face in the ring. One former WWE performer that did speak out against Trump, Maria Kanellis, returned to the company in 2017, as part of a tandem with her husband, Mike Bennett, though both were later released in April, 2020.

At the GOP convention, Trump received twenty-eight delegate nominations from Connecticut. It is not uncommon for a state party's chairman to brag about his or her state while announcing the delegation.

Connecticut chairman J.R. Romano took particular delight in his announcement: "Well, Mister Chairman, I come from the land where we manufacture PEZ, nuclear submarines and the home of WWE, where men are men and women are champions. The great state of Connecticut casts all 28 delegates for the next president of the United States, Donald J. Trump." Linda McMahon served as a delegate for Trump.

Trump's extensive time with the McMahons and in the world of WWE was not lost on him during a contentious GOP debate season. In a collegial interview with Sean Hannity, Hannity said the debate format felt a bit like WWE in that there was a lot of finger pointing and name calling. Trump's response referenced WWE and McMahon, as well: "It was a little bit like WWE, the great Vince McMahon—who is a *terrific* guy—the way every question had to do with me . . . 'Mr. Trump said this,' 'Mr. Trump said that.'"

James Poniewozik, author of *Audience of One: Donald Trump, Television, and the fracturing of America*, said that Trump is "not a person." "He's a character that wrote itself, a brand mascot that jumped off the cereal box and into the world."

During the campaign Trump utilized a familiar wrestling trope of assigning simple and memorable nicknames and buzzwords to opponents that would stick with the public. Those included nicknames like "Crooked Hilary" for Hillary Clinton and "Little Marco" for Marco Rubio, and Jeb Bush as "Low Energy," the latter of which gained mainstream popularity on national social media networks.

The Honky Tonk Man, from WrestleMania IV, speculated that McMahon was suggesting some of the insults to Trump. Supporters enjoyed the phrases, especially as they related to Hillary Clinton. Chants of "Lock her up!" could be heard at most Trump rallies.

Linda McMahon was on hand for a Trump's rally

in Fairfield, Connecticut at Sacred Heart University's William H. Pitt Center on August 13th, 2016 and met with Trump backstage. McMahon served as the vice chairperson of the board of trustees for the college. Sacred Heart distanced itself from the event. Deborah Noack stated that it is not a university sponsored event and should not imply endorsement of any kind. A connection was made by Trump's state director to Linda McMahon for a campus contact to facilitate the event.

Many were surprised that Trump would rally in the state, given dim hopes for a Republican candidate and Obama's prior wins by wide margins. Trump thanked Linda McMahon that evening and took the time to slam Richard Blumenthal (along with his many other perceived ills of the state): "He went around for years saying he was a great Vietnam fighter, telling false [tales], telling everything. Linda exposed him- and he got elected? How the hell do you elect a guy like that?" Domonik Boehner was in attendance to support Trump: "He's a little loud with his mouth but most Americans are. He doesn't speak that political mumbo jumbo." The last time a Republican Presidential candidate had won the state was 1988, when George H.W. Bush defeated Michael Dukakis. Hillary Clinton would carry the state with a 54.57 percent (897,572 votes) to 40.93 percent (673,215 votes) margin.

Vice described attendees at a Trump rally as men in their middle ages, smoking and walking around in what looked like homemade wrestling costumes. Matt Taibi explains in *Hate Inc.: Why Today's Media Makes Us Despise One Another*, where the press went wrong in not understanding what was happening: "The campaign press played the shocked commentator in perfect deadpan, in part because they were genuinely clueless about what they were doing. They never understood that the proper way to "cover" pro wrestling, if you're being serious, is to not cover it."

One could say that Trump rallies had the feel of a raucous wrestling crowd, albeit one that hadn't watched since the heyday of the Rock, or Hulk Hogan. National media was quick to pick up on the similarities between Trump's campaign and the world of WWE. Most visually connected to Trump's pro wrestling roots was his entrance at the Republican National Convention. Queen's hit song "We Are The Champions" played, while the convention floor lights were dimmed. Trump was first visible in silhouette, bathed in blue light. He clapped for himself before stepping up to the microphone to introduce his wife, Melania. The entrance was compared by fans to that of WWE mainstay, the Undertaker. Trump did not deny the connection to pro wrestling, noting his connection to Vince. As Sean Illing at *Vox* described, "Donald Trump is the show we can't turn off, the car crash we can't look away from, the news cycle we can't escape." Trump later said that McMahon called him and complimented the entrance.

David Brooks of *The New York Times* was skeptical of Trump's chances but had a sense of where he was coming from: "I still don't think the spectacle is going to carry Trump to the White House." He described his campaign of taking working class manners (or "proletarian," as Brooks put it) from professional wrestling and placing them into the world of presidential politics. Brooks in assessing the temperature of the nation felt that people were angry, had lost faith and felt powerless. There had to be a leader whose confrontational abilities would be a win in and of itself. Trump represented the people who felt downtrodden and fought against social inequality. How Brooks could be so insightful but not see Trump as having an actual chance to win is unclear.

Emmert Dose of *The Journal Times* in Racine, Wisconsin, in his September 2015 column was the better prognosticator: "What, you don't think Trump will be elected President? Remember, retired wrestler Jesse Ventura was elected Governor of Minnesota." A.J. Nino Amato in *The Capital Times* felt that one reason Trump's chances should be taken very seriously are because of the "Jesse Ventura Effect": An increase in voters who want to shake up established politics due to their frustrations.

Gene Lyons, in a column in the *Santa Maria Times* speculated that the version of pro wrestling that Trump was drawing his inspiration from was not from the recent past, what he may have observed from the front row, but what he'd have watched on television in his childhood from the WWWF, then run by Vince McMahon Sr. That promotion was "all about ethnicity and race" according to him. Varying ethnic groups were present, representing the best (and often worst) of stereotypical representations of men who'd immigrated from those countries.

Perhaps the most inspirational character to Trump was Dr. Jerry Graham, the cocky heel with the peroxide blonde hair. One man that was definitely enamored with Graham was Vince McMahon, Jr.: "Oh, boy. It's 1959 and I'm looking up at Jerry Graham and he's lighting cigars with $100 bills . . . he wore red shoes and rode around Washington in a blood-red 1959 Cadillac, smoking a cigar. He'd run red lights, blowing the horn, and people would scatter. If they didn't get out of his way he'd cut a promo." McMahon's father was not pleased. The younger McMahon would have to sneak away to go on joyrides with Graham.

Hulk Hogan did not want to miss out on the opportunity to connect himself to Trump. Upon prompting by a *TMZ* reporter as to which candidate Hogan would like to face in a match, Hogan threw his hat in the ring as a potential Trump running mate early in the GOP race. Hogan had been fired by WWE not too much earlier for being linked to racist recordings (he used the "N" word) related to his daughter dating an African-American man. Jerry Lawler felt that there was an overreaction to the controversy. Hogan was not necessarily tied closely to one political party or another. Hogan supported Romney during the 2012 election and Obama in 2008.

Jesse Ventura also threw his hat in the ring as a potential running mate for Trump. At the same time, he was also considering his own run for President through the Liberterian party: "I would challenge the American people to make history with me." Ventura said that he would give an invitation to be Vice President a very serious consideration (despite not being asked) as the country needed a shake-up.

Ventura, in discussing Trump's political aspirations in 2016, encouraged Trump to be on the offensive and said that Trump was speaking from the heart and just speaking the truth. Ventura and Trump's views were not exactly aligned at this time but Ventura did not see that as an insurmountable barrier: "I'd be there to fight him over that (military intervention in the Middle East) and show him why it's an idiotic policy to begin with." He also denounced Trump's policies on immigration on his internet show (a show he does not watch as he said, "I don't do the internet"). Ventura had an odd reason to be chosen: "You got to pick someone who is worse than you to ensure your safety."

Unfortunately for Ventura, his political star had fallen greatly since his surprise run as the Governor, conspiracy theories and all, and he was unlikely to be given any serious consideration as a Vice Presidential candidate by Trump, even with a non-traditional approach to the political process.

Ventura did not run himself either and ultimately chose to endorse Gary Johnson, the Libertarian candidate and Governor of New Mexico. In a swerve, Ventura voted for someone else: Dr. Jill Stein of the Green Party.

Jerry "The King" Lawler appealed to voters in New Hampshire to support Donald Trump in the primaries. He realized that this was not the best idea when he received death threats and said he planned to stay out of politics. Jerry Lawler noted that he received hundreds of obscene tweets from Hillary supporters. Lawler apparently did not learn enough about the political landmines in running previously for Mayor of Memphis, Tennessee.

Linda McMahon's Connecticut primary opponent in 2012, Christopher Shays saw similarities in the candidates: "Trump has the celebrity status, not unlike what we saw in the State of Connecticut with Linda McMahon." Shays continued, "What will ultimately be his death knell will be that he has incredibly high negatives, like Linda McMahon." What Shays did learn that proved true in running against McMahon is that "Celebrity status is huge."

Donald Trump was elected President of the United States in November 2016 in perhaps the most shocking presidential victory since the first ballot was cast and arguably the biggest political shock since Jesse Ventura was given little chance of winning the election for Governor of Minnesota in 1998.

CNN referred to Trump as "Body Slammer in Chief." Shares of WWE were up seven percent following Trump's election. The official Donald Trump profile page on WWE.com was updated to include the election results: "After trading in his favorite television catchphrase "You're fired!" for a national promise to "Make America Great Again," Donald Trump won his first presidential campaign against key contender Hillary Clinton and officially took the oath of office on January 20, 2017, to become the 45th President of the United States—the first time in history a WWE Hall of Fame inductee would hold the distinguished title of Commander in Chief."

Stephanie McMahon Levesque described Trump in glowing words, shortly after the election: "We've done a lot with Donald Trump over the years. He's been a great supporter of WWE; he's been a great friend to us. We've had events at his building. He's been a participant at WrestleMania," she said. "It's great to see him have the success he is having."

Paul Levesque, McMahon's son-in-law expressed cautious optimism at Trump's election. He stated that they, the extended McMahon family, would be waiting to see what Donald Trump as President meant for the country and the world. Levesque felt it was great to see the success Trump was now experiencing. Levesque reiterated WWE's strong relationship with Trump over the years, including him hosting events, being an active participant in company storylines, and joining the Hall of Fame.

The response on Twitter from wrestlers to the election results was mixed but mostly reserved. Wrestler Sasha Banks responded with three sad emojis. Austin Watson, a member of The New Day known as Xavier

Woods, responded with a sad looking emoji as well. His on-screen teammate, Kofi Kingston of The New Day wrote: "Welp, here we go . . . " Renee Young, an on-air broadcaster, noted that it "didn't feel real."

Sami Zayn, a Canadian born WWE star of Syrian descent, considered the election results a horrible night and compared the results to Nazi Germany. He later tweeted about the Muslim travel ban: "I can't articulate how truly disgusted I am right now." Interestingly, Zayn is a rare WWE Superstar with Middle Eastern roots who has never been portrayed by the company in a stereotypical manner such as an anti-American aggressor or a terrorist. The WWE had been smartly gun-shy for years about running such storylines since airing a martyr angle on Smackdown on the now defunct UPN Network. The pre-taped show aired the day after a terrorist bombing in London. Mark Copani, an Arab-American known on-screen as Muhammad Hassan, was taken off the network and released by the company a few months later.

Trump also had supporters in the wrestling community. WWE wrestler Bubba Ray Dudley, part of long-time on-again, off-again WWE tag team mainstays the Dudley Boyz, was quick to join the "media are liars" camp, saying that the media predicted the wrong results because the various outlets have been lying every step of the way. He also joked about Bill Clinton needing to contact Monica Lewinsky that night. John Layfield, now a WWE commentator and occasional Fox News business analyst, called on everyone to stop the name calling and just get along. WWE announcer Corey Graves focused on an important issue during the election: helping those in need, such as welfare services. Graves, invoking an often played trope when mentioning those on the lower rung of the financial scale, said that he was once on welfare but "worked his ass off" and got to where he is. He didn't need a President's help, and by that logic, seemingly no one else would either.

Former Trump Battle of the Billionaires representative Bobby Lashley seemed to be one of the few who found humor in the win. He reminded everyone to be civil and linked to a picture of Hillary Clinton in the barber's chair, in a Photoshopped picture from WrestleMania 23, with Hillary as a stand-in for Vince McMahon.

In a comment to the *Star Tribune* of Minnesota, reader Lily Chua O'Conner lent some perspective to those upset by the news: "Remember, we survived four years of Jesse Ventura."

Surprisingly to some, WWE has managed to almost avoid referencing Donald Trump in storylines thus far. Frederick Douglas Rosser III, known as Darren Young, participated in a storyline entitled "Make Darren Young Great Again." Bob Backlund, playing up his real-life interest in motivational speaking, was placed as an on-air life coach for Young in May of 2016. Young had spent the majority of his career in mid-card roles. Young was most famous to the general public for coming out as a gay person, a significant moment as the first active WWE wrestler to come out publicly. The storyline, like most of Young's career, was met with apathy by the fans and drew little resemblance to the Trump campaign, outside of a similar catchphrase.

To Backlund, it was only partly storyline. In an interview with *Ring Rust Radio*, he explained his determination to meet Trump. Backlund said that he had visited The White House and Trump Tower in an attempt to meet Trump (it appeared that both appearances were at Backlund's own accord and not invitations).

Backlund wanted to be part of an initiative to make America great by speaking in schools and explaining the importance of hard work. Backlund said that he was inspired by Trump's words to him when they were both honored at the Hall of Fame induction ceremony. Backlund said that Trump told him that Backlund could light up all of New York City with his energy. At the event,

Backlund had to be cut off as his speech went well past the allotted time and he showed no signs of slowing down. Vince McMahon himself had to come out to signal Backlund off the stage. McMahon tip-toed out with his fingers over his lips. Backlund then screamed into the microphone, "I'm done!" Backlund was, of course, not done and a minute later, Levesque had to help escort Backlund off the stage.

Politics have leaked into indie wrestling, as well. Appalachian Mountain Wrestling featured a villain wrestler known as the "Progressive Liberal" Daniel Richards. His uniform of choice? A t-shirt with various faces of Trump's greatest outside the ring rival, Hillary Clinton, covering the shirt from top to bottom. His finisher is known as the "Liberal Agenda." His form-fitting wrestling bottoms have images of a donkey, most associated with the Democratic Party. It has given fans of Trump, in one of his strongholds of support, someone to boo. According to WBIR radio, Trump received fifty-nine percent of the vote in the presidential election in Knox County, Tennessee as compared with Hilary Clinton at thirty-five percent.

On one particular night, wrestling was in town, and the "Progressive Liberal" called Trump a con man in a speech to the fans. The crowd booed in unison and a fan told him to shut up. While fans found the villain easy to jeer, media with a more liberal slant looked on with amusement and astonishment. Outlets with more liberal readers like the *Washington Post* and *Deadline* tried to get a better handle on what is going on in East Tennessee.

In the *New York Times*, Nick Rogers, a lawyer and sociologist, wrote an op-ed piece attempting to understand Trump and Alex Jones of InfoWars infamy, invoked a long-time wrestling insider term. "Kayfabe" refers to protecting the business and staying in character. For example, if two wrestlers are discussing the business and an outsider appears within earshot, a wrestler will announce "Kayfabe!," a cue to keep your mouth shut or change the subject.

Rogers somewhat missed the point in describing the term as an agreement that the performers will present something fake and the fans will agree to lose themselves in the form of entertainment, a definition from Rogers almost opposite to how the term was intended. Rogers used the kayfabe lens to highlight Trump and his supporters' line of thinking: Trump may present facts that are factually inaccurate, but his supporters (or fans) will agree not to question it as it is something that they want to believe.

Poniewozik, in *Audience of One*, explains that wrestling fans could buy into professional wrestling at whatever level they wanted: Yes, it's scripted, but the emotion may be real and this is also true of politics from a Trumpian lens:

It's not so much about being taken in or thinking he's totally honest, it's about this guy who's fighting for your side. And even if there's this level of bullshit and artifice, it's only because he's a clever trickster. And besides, what's most important is how he makes his voters feel.

One of the only performers who was in the position to speak more freely would be the biggest modern- day star of the company, John Cena. In an appearance on *The Kyle & Jackie O Show* in Sydney, Australia, Cena was asked his thoughts. Appearing a bit more nervous than usual, Cena acknowledged it was a difficult question but said that Trump could be extremely abrasive. He didn't think that the controversy surrounding the President was good for anyone. Cena said that time will tell as to how we ultimately judge Trump. On an episode of *Today*, Cena expressed concerns for a plan to ban Muslims from entering the country. He compared the political agenda to what happened during World War II and said Trump was being Trump. Cena starred in an official WWE video related to patriotism and diversity on the weekend of July 4, 2016, when the nation was caught up in a contentious election season and debate about different types of people. He encouraged viewers to consider the varied types of Americans and to show love beyond labels.

Some fans considered participating in a boycott of WWE because of Trump's long-standing connections to the McMahons and the company. The boycott would consist of cancelling WWE Network subscriptions, not tuning into *Monday Night Raw*, and not attending live WWE arena events when it comes to town. At the end of the day, any boycott may have been partaken by individual fans or small pockets of fans who have chosen to no longer support the company but it does not appear to have had any significant influence upon business. The #boycottWWE hashtag on Twitter had been more likely used as a protest by fans to voice disapproval of a star they do not support, such as Roman Reigns, getting more airtime than one of their favorites than it is to be used against a Trump policy. At the end of the day, most fans did not want to give up something that brings pleasure to their lives and serves as a distraction from the everyday stresses of life. One fan was photographed among protesters outside Trump Tower when the president was in town. His sign read *WRESTLING FANS AGAINST TRUMP* and featured a crude drawing of Austin using the stunner on Trump.

Once the Presidential votes were in and it was clear Donald Trump would be our next President, Linda McMahon tweeted words of congratulations: "What a night! Thrilled to congratulate my friend, President-Elect Donald Trump on a hard-fought campaign and victory."

As early as November 2016, Linda McMahon was being considered for the role of the Secretary of Commerce. In December, Linda met with Trump in New York's Trump Tower. She made it clear to the press that she was not interested in an Ambassadorship and said to "Stay tuned," when asked if she was offered a position in the forthcoming administration.

In December 2016, Linda McMahon was named as the Administrator of the Small Business Administration [SBA], a cabinet-level position. Trump stated that McMahon "has a tremendous background and is widely recognized as one of the country's top female executives advising businesses around the globe. She helped grow WWE from a modest thirteen-person operation to a publicly traded global enterprise with more than 800 employees in offices worldwide. Linda is going to be a phenomenal leader and champion for small businesses and unleash America's entrepreneurial spirit across the country." McMahon said that she shares Trump's vision of decreasing "burdensome regulations that are hurting our middle-class workers and small businesses." She further told reporters regarding Trump, "Once you're his friend, he is loyal to the end . . . He's an incredibly loyal, loyal friend." McMahon's nomination was considered part of Trump's "billionaire's row" as described by the *Hartford Courant*, which included Betsy Devos, Vincent Viola, Todd Ricketts and Wilbur Ross.

In preparation of her confirmation, McMahon planned to divest of several positions and assets. This would include stepping down as the vice chairwoman of the Board of Trustees at Sacred Heart University. As it related to WWE, McMahon would not "participate personally and substantially in any particular matter that to my knowledge has a direct and predictable effect on the financial interests of the World Wrestling Entertainment, Inc., unless I first obtain a written waiver."

Stephanie McMahon Levesque, daughter of Vince and Linda, and her husband, Paul Levesque, were in attendance for Trump's inauguration. She tweeted: "Regardless your politics, it was an honor to witness the peaceful transition of power as our 45th President was inaugurated. #ProudToBeAmerican"

Why Stephanie thought that the transition of power would not be peaceful was unclear.

Stephanie and Paul returned to Washington D.C.

to observe Linda's hearing before Congress on January 24, 2017. Linda was unanimously approved, at a count of 16–0, by the US Senate Small Business Committee. In February, the Senate confirmed McMahon's appointment by a vote of 81–19. Surprisingly, during the hearings little was mentioned about WWE's track record of classifying their full-time performers as "independent contractors" and not employees, thus limiting the type of benefits that workers receive, such as healthcare. Additionally, there was little mention of WWE's aggressive expansion plans in the early 1980s, that resulted in several regional wrestling territories (or, small businesses) going out of business.

Senator Tammy Duckworth, a Democrat from Illinois, was the only elected official who mentioned related concerns during the hearings. However, she did not publicly question McMahon on the issues. Senator Duckworth said that in their one-on-one meeting the previous day, she had expressed concern about WWE's use of 1099s (independent contractor status) related to the health of performers as well as her concerns about WWE's monopolistic practices. Senator Duckworth then moved on to ask an unrelated question, meaning an opportunity was lost for Ms. McMahon to address these important issues under oath.

The senators invited Ms. McMahon to visit their states, seemingly unfamiliar that Linda had probably been to their states already in her role with WWE. The Associated Press speculated that based upon how the hearings proceeded, she should comfortably win confirmation. McMahon, once confirmed, did embark on a sixty-eight city schedule to visit each of SBA's offices.

Democratic Senators were said to be impressed that McMahon received endorsements from her Connecticut political rivals of 2010 and 2012. Richard Blumenthal praised Linda for utilizing her business to help women and veterans. In 2010, Blumenthal had said that McMahon was one to put profits ahead of people and hire lobbyists to negate regulation of professional wrestling. Blumenthal would later be eviscerated by Trump on Twitter over the controversy about the nature of Blumenthal's service during Vietnam.

McMahon met with her other former rival in Connecticut, Senator Chris Murphy in Washington. Things went well as Murphy stated to the *Hartford Courant* that she is a "talented and experienced businessperson, there's no doubt about it." And in a line that couldn't have been said better if McMahon or WWE PR wrote it themselves: "She helped shepherd WWE from a mere idea into an incredibly successful enterprise. . . ."

By 2017, there was some friction between Connecticut Democrats and Trump. One name that was speculated on as a bridge between representatives like Blumenthal and Murphy was Linda. Gary Rose of Sacred Heart stated: "I don't think you are going to see the congresspersons and the two senators working closely with Trump and helping our state. It's really going to be Linda."

McMahon discussed how she had built her business from scratch and even shared a desk with her husband, Vince. The McMahons had been so strapped at one point, McMahon claimed, that she rented a typewriter. McMahon acknowledged declaring bankruptcy in the past and how that better informed her to understand small business. McMahon explained how she did not expect employees to do anything she would not do herself. Senator Mazie Hirono, a Democrat from Hawaii, praised McMahon for addressing the negative comments about women made by Trump during the presidential race. McMahon did not address the praise as she likely hoped to move on from that period of time.

Most speakers at the confirmation hearings thanked McMahon for her time in meeting with them privately, a strategy which seemed to allay any concerns about her candidacy. Stephanie McMahon and Paul Levesque can be seen on camera during the telecast while Linda discussed her prepared statements. Linda asked Stephanie and Paul to stand up and uncharacteristically, they did so, albeit hesitantly. The presence of McMahon's daughter and son-in-law seemed to have made a real impression on the senators, as they mentioned McMahon's family several times.

As with Linda's testimony on deregulation in New Jersey and Pennsylvania, Vince was not in attendance. Heidi Heitkamp, a democrat from North Dakota mentioned that she "had seen the pride and affection in your daughter's face. I wish you could see that affection." Stephanie appeared to be glowing after the hearing concluded, seemingly proud of her mom and almost overwhelmed to tears by the moment.

As with any diverse crowd, there were certainly WWE fans among the elected officials. Tim Ernst, a Republican from South Carolina, made special effort to name drop Triple H and The Rock in the form of a joke. Awkwardly, no one laughed until Ernst explained that he was making a joke. Ernst discussed how he had been a fan of the National Wrestling Alliance (NWA), one of McMahon's primary competitors. The Carolinas have long been called "Flair Country" after Ric Flair, as he and the

NWA often drew some of their biggest box offices there in the past. The Carolinas were a wrestling stronghold until WWE became the dominant promotion in the country. Today, South Carolina, is not a regular stop on the current WWE tour circuit.

Cory Booker, a Democrat from New Jersey, joked that Stephanie McMahon looked fiercer than her husband. He mentioned that Levesque seemed to be slipping in his workout routines. Linda confirmed that Stephanie can deliver "a mean hip toss." He did not vote to confirm McMahon for the role in the end, but one of his opponents in the 2020 democratic race, Amy Klobuchar, did.

Rod Blum, a representative from Iowa, asked McMahon why it had taken John Cena so long to get engaged to fellow performer Stephanie Garcia-Colace, known as Niki Bella. McMahon responded that you would have to ask him. The answer was that Cena and Bella had been waiting for the right public moment: WrestleMania, which occurred just a few days earlier (the couple would break up before getting married). McMahon sat front row in Washington, D.C with her grandkids when WWE rolled into town on July 24, 2017.

The extended McMahon family—children and grandchildren included—took part in a photo opportunity with the President in the Oval Office on the day Linda was sworn in. Her six grandchildren also surrounded McMahon during part of the swearing-in ceremony, including holding the bible up for her while she took the oath. Making the photo unique was one of McMahon's granddaughters holding up a photo taken at WrestleMania 23 showing Trump shaving McMahon's head. The photo was provided as a gift to Trump. Additionally, Vince and Linda took an individual photo with Trump in the Oval Office.

Linda McMahon spent $100,000,000 in two runs to secure a senate nomination in Connecticut. Ironically, it was her old friend, Donald Trump, that finally provided her with the clout and political appointment she had been seeking for so many years. Levesque told CNBC that he was proud of Linda and, in a bit of an overstatement, said that she would be a great fit for the SBA as WWE (as WWWF) had been a tiny company in the Northeastern United States before she (and Vince) took over.

McMahon's appointment made for good fodder in a column by Gail Collins of *The New York Times*, a tongue-in-cheek quiz writer: How well do you remember the year that was? In reference to 2016. McMahon was the subject of the seventh question:

Question 7) Linda McMahon, Trump's pick for the head of the Small Business Administration, has known the President-elect a long time. McMahon's husband Vince, once paired with Trump in a . . .

a) Professional wrestling production in which Trump shaved off McMahon's hair.

b) Build-the-Wall golf match in which they could see who could hit the most golf balls into Mexico.

c) Public service announcements warning young men about steroid abuse.

Along with other Trump officials, such as Steve Mnuchin and Gary Cohen, Linda moved into the Trump International Hotel in Washington D.C. upon her appointment. The location was just a few blocks from the White House and housed in the Old Post Office building. Lobbyists and foreign leaders made the effort to spend time at the hotel to curry favor with the president.

Notably, in 2018, the hotel was best known for the projected signage on the front. In addition to the expected words Trump, "shithole," with poop emojis took up the majority of the real estate. This was a cheeky reference to Trump's classification of Haiti and the African continent.

The Detroit Free Press speculated that Trump

could learn from McMahon in building bridges and establishing relationships. Smartly for remaining in the good graces of the President, McMahon provided a politically safe answer when asked by the paper in August of 2017 what she thought about the presidency thus far. McMahon responded that she had been quite busy traveling and that she had not had the time to pay attention to what Trump was saying. She did say that he was a smart businessperson and that he was dedicated to a more efficient government. The paper was impressed that McMahon did not mention anything about "fake news" and focused on the facts.

On Tuesday, August 1 2017, Linda McMahon participated in her highest profile event thus far as Administrator of the Small Business Administration. In the East Room of the White House, McMahon flanked Donald Trump on one side, while Senior Advisor Ivanka Trump flanked Donald on the other, in welcoming attendees to the "Engine of the American Dream" event. Trump reminded everyone that he had known Linda for a long time and that she and her husband had built an incredible business. Later, McMahon and Ivanka sat together and fielded questions from the small business owners in attendance.

Despite McMahon's newest role outside of

WWE, she could not escape the shadow of the wrestling community. The Pro Wrestling Torch, a long running insider newsletter and website, ran a poll regarding McMahon's appointment to Trump's cabinet: "Does Linda McMahon being in a cabinet position with President Trump affect your desire to support WWE?" There were 435 total votes. Forty-nine percent choose "No, it probably doesn't affect it at all"; Forty-two percent answered "Yes, I might support WWE less"; and nine percent answered, "Yes, I might support WWE more."

In honor of Black History Month, on February 2017, WWE aired a video on *Monday Night Raw* paying tribute to Barack Obama. Several African American "WWE Superstars" (corporate jargon for male wrestlers) spoke glowingly of his achievements.

Despite busy days and nights as the 45th President of the United States, Trump remained nostalgic about his pro wrestling roots. Twitter is Trump's preferred method of communication as he enjoys the unfiltered nature this form of communication allows given he feels that he is at odds with many members of the media. Trump was happy to thank John Bradshaw Layfield in a tweet on April 1, 2017 when Layfield noted a rise in consumer confidence during an appearance as a financial analyst on Fox News.

Trump and Vince McMahon are fairly choosy about who they "follow" on Twitter with only a handful of follows each but have chosen to follow each other. In July, Trump tweeted: "Fraud News CNN, #FNN." The hashtags were followed by a video of Donald Trump's thrashing of McMahon at WrestleMania XXIII. The only difference was McMahon's head was replaced by the CNN logo. *The New York Times* described the video as an unorthodox way for the President to portray himself and said the video was the quality of a cartoon. Liberal-leaning members of Twitter were quick to respond with a meme of their own: The President receiving a "Stone Cold Stunner" at the end of the match. Even CNN jumped in, tweeting with a tongue in cheek video, about getting bullied by Trump.

The controversy continued as it came out that the video was made by a Reddit user named "HanAssholeSolo." Jerry "The King" Lawler, Trump's long-time supporter in WWE, was quick to jump in: "Pretty cool to be a commentator on a tweet from the President!"

Vince McMahon knows that to top a record setting WrestleMania, you need to return the next time with a bigger main event. Days after the election, there were rumors that Trump could return one day to face McMahon in a return of the Battle of the Billionaires. McMahon's son-in-law, Levesque, said that it would be something to see who gets their head shaved in another high stakes matchup. But as CNBC wrote in a headline, don't count on it. More referring to his Republican National Convention wrestling like entrance, but possibly shedding light onto why he has yet to, and may never, repeat the Battle of the Billionaires, Trump stated that doing something a second time never works out as well. However, Trump did participate in a similar entrance during a rally in June of 2020 in Tulsa, Oklahoma.

A survey was administered by *The Washington Post* and the University of Massachusetts Lowell in August 2017 to learn about American's view of sports. Tied with esports for the least popular sport was professional wrestling while American football came in first. The poll provided insight into political partisan support among sports fans. By the widest margin, pro wrestling fans identified as Democratic. While most sports favored Democratic support, hockey and auto racing favored Republican.

George Herbert Walker Bush died on November 30, 2018. WWE happened to be in Houston, Texas on the following Monday, December 3. On its *Raw* program, it paid tribute to the fallen for President with a ten-bell salute.

WWE benefited from a strengthening of relationships between the United States and Saudi Arabia. Prince Mohammed bin Salman bin Abdulaziz al-Saud, or MBS, for short, had recently risen to power (or consolidated power to himself) and was seeking to bring a certain modern veneer to the country- such as allowing women to drive- and a different perspective to the outside world. One of those people he'd established a relationship with was Donald Trump's son-in-law, Jared Kusher. According to Ben Hubbard in his book MBS, they'd often exchange communication over WhatsApp, outside of more traditional communication channels.

A major initiative undertaken by MBS was the creation of Vision 2030, a plan to move away from the country's reliance on oil for the economy and diversify to a number of industries, including tourism. This is where WWE came in, along with, as Hubbard would describe it, a "royal populist appeal," through various forms of entertainment to young people including pro wrestling. A lower profile WWE tour in Saudi Arabia in 2014 featured only male performers and may have been the first WWE show with a completely male audience (or at least in many years).

The WWE was provided with a large guaranteed sum of money to come to the country in a ten-year agreement as part of Vision 2030 and perform while bringing greater attention and legitimacy to the host—not unlike the company's WrestleMania IV and V appearances in Atlantic City for Trump. Vince McMahon and Paul Levesque represented WWE in flying to the country to close the deal and al-Sheikh, the Chairman of the Authority represented Saudi Arabia. In addition to live events, the deal would include WWE Network, digital, social media and television-related promotion/distribution. Vince McMahon said: "The Greatest Royal Rumble will be a spectacle of historical proportions. Our partnership with the Saudi General Sports Authority reflects a long-term commitment to present WWE's world-class entertainment to a global audience on a grander scale than ever before."

Seating was determined by the Saudi hosts. Families were allotted seats closer to the ring. Single men had to sit farther back. It led to some complaints as there were sections of family seats that did not sell immediately, and single men would have liked to have been able to purchase those seats.

On the same week that AMC opened its first movie theater in Riyadh with Black Panther, the WWE event, The Greatest Royal Rumble on April 27, 2018, showed beautiful aerial views of the city of Jeddah at the King Abdullah Sports City Stadium with an estimated 47,000-50,000 in attendance.

A two-minute video played during the broadcast that included the following in narrator voice: "It's the dawning of a new age in Saudi Arabia. And the societal renaissance that is sweeping this great nation has a great deal to do with thirty-two-year-old Crown Prince, Mohamed Bin Salman." The announcers talked up the various sites to see and John Cena talked about how fortunate he felt to be there.

Women did not perform on the show, although they were reported to have received a payment of some kind following the event. Those paying close attention to world events were appalled given a history of Saudi Arabia's human rights violations. Its ongoing war in Yemen has included bombings of school children on buses and hospitals, and it has been described by some as the world's biggest humanitarian crisis.

Paul Levesque attempted to explain some of the tradeoffs necessary for the event: "While, right now, women are not competing in the event, we have had discussions about that and we believe and hope that in the next few years, they will be. That is a significant cultural shift in Saudi Arabia. The country is in the middle of a shift in how it is dealing with that—the position is changing, and rights are changing, as are the way women are handled and treated in society. We think that's a great thing and we're excited to be at the forefront of that change."

There was a curious story emerging from the event that the Saudi side, with only a cursory knowledge of the company's performers, had specifically requested that Yokozuna appear at the event. Unfortunately, he had died several years before. Rather than disappoint, the company found an actual sumo wrestler as a stand-in: Hiroki Sumi. He did not impress in the Royal Rumble portion of the evening.

This is not to say the event was not without controversy in its home country as well. When a promotional video aired showing Sasha Banks and Carmella (in a Baywatch like bathing suit) in an advertisement for WWE's forthcoming Backlash event, some male fans in the audience cheered. The General Sports Authority had to issue an apology (translated below):

> *"The General Sport Authority would like to apologize to the viewers and attendees of last night's WWE event that took place in Jeddah, over the indecent scene involving women that appeared as an ad before a segment. It would*

like to confirm its total disapproval of this, in the shadow of its commitment to eliminate anything that goes against the community's values.

The authority has made sure to ban showing of any segment that involves women wrestling or any scenes related to it and stipulated that to the company (WWE). The authority also disapproved any promotional stuff with pictures or videos showing women in an indecent way and emphasized on commitment of this rule. And it's a commitment that the authority would still commit to forever in all of its events and programs."

The company wrote a localized storyline for the show in Jeddah. Iran, Saudi Arabia's regional rival, was at the center of a storyline where the Daivari Brothers came out waving the Iranian flag, then were run off by four Saudi Arabian wrestlers. After the show, Ariya Daviari received death threats.

During an appearance this past Friday, I portrayed a fictional character and played the role of the antagonist, no different than what other actors would do in a movie or TV show. That character does not reflect my personal viewers and I apologize to anyone that may have been offended by the skit. I have an incredible amount of respect for the great people of Iran and I am very proud of my Iranian heritage.

All in all, WWE got away mostly unscathed by the controversy and found a significant revenue source to its bottom line until a larger controversy hit. Jamal Khashoggi, a Saudi national and journalist for *The Washington Post* living abroad, was murdered in the Saudi consulate in Turkey on October 2nd, 2018. He had entered the consulate to obtain a marriage license, but he never exited. He was suffocated and his body was sliced into parts by men who'd travelled from Saudi Arabia, knowing he'd be arriving that day. Khashoggi had been critical of the regime. MBS denied knowledge of what happened, despite evidence to the controversy. Many corporations began attempting to distance themselves from doing business with the country. With WWE having an upcoming "Crown Jewel" event, there was some speculation the company would cancel but only if the state department or President Trump mandated it.

No order to cancel the event transpired. In its quarterly report, WWE addressed the controversy and its plans to move forward: "Considering the heinous crime committed at the Saudi consulate in Istanbul, the company faced a very difficult decision as it relates to its event scheduled for Nov. 2 in Riyadh. Similar to other US-based companies who plan to continue operations in Saudi

Arabia, the company has decided to uphold its contractual obligations."

In November, the President came out in support of Saudi Arabia, claiming "The world is a dangerous place!" John Bolton revealed in his book *The Room Where It Happened*, that this was meant as a distraction from the fact that Ivanka was under scrutiny for using private emails to contact government officials using ijkfamily.com (a similar situation to Hillary Clinton using a private email server that inspired the "Lock Her Up" chants). One of those officials was Linda McMahon. She wrote to Linda in 2017, a year prior, that they should explore possible "opportunities to collaborate."

WWE did become more conservative in mentioning of the 2018 Crown Jewel event, only naming the event on air but avoiding the country and city wherever possible. When the city was mentioned, the country was often omitted. Fans attending live shows stateside booed when promotional videos appeared on the screen for Crown Jewel. John Cena who stated he was so proud to be at the Greatest Royal Rumble, would decline participation in this event and any additional events in the country.

Lindsey Graham, in a rare break from President Trump, suggested that there should be a rethinking of

America's relationship with Saudi Arabia and a pause on WWE's planned event.

Richard Blumenthal, the Connecticut Senator who has a complicated relationship with Linda McMahon stated "All major private interests should review and relook at their relationship with the Saudi Kingdom in light of its continuing pattern of abuse of civil rights and civil liberties, contempt for the rule of law, and bombing in Yemen using the US military equipment and possible intelligence." Blumenthal had no plans to pressure WWE but hoped that "WWE will recognize on its own a conscience and conviction if there is proof that Saudi official approved and ordered this kind of killing, and I would lean first on the United States government to do its duty so that it can lead private interests like WWE, and the first place to look is the United States of America."

Hulk Hogan did return to the company fold at the event. The groundwork had been laid before in Hogan's volunteer work: "WWE applauds the work Hulk Hogan is doing with Boys & Girls Clubs of America to turn what was a negative into a positive by helping young people learn from his mistake. While he has taken many steps in the right direction since we parted ways, Hogan' is not currently under contract to WWE."

WWE was allowed to bring its first female on air

talent (but not a wrestler), Renee Young. The event broadcast felt different as Riyadh was mentioned but not Saudi Arabia or MBS. There was no on-air praise of the country.

Following the event, it was speculated that Linda McMahon may replace Wilbur Ross as the Commerce Secretary. McMahon was asked if WWE should return to Saudi Arabia and she deflected it well as always, stating that she would not be the person to talk to on that subject.

WWE's overall relationship was panned by some of wrestling's most ardent fans. In the year end *Wrestling Observer Awards*, Crown Jewel was voted the Worst Wrestling Show, and the Most Disgusting Promotional Tactic Award went to WWE for "business ties with Saudi Arabia," which won the category in the following year, as well.

October of 2019 brought word of another twist in the WWE—Saudi Arabia relationship. Crown Jewel show that year had its live feed in the country delayed for forty minutes by Vince McMahon. In a meeting with management, talent was told that the delay was due to a technical issue.

It was reported that the company was still owed money from previous shows and was using the live event as leverage. Wrestlers were delayed for six hours on the tarmac in what had been reported by the company as "mechanical issues" but it was felt that it was part of a game between the two parties. Atlas Air issued a statement that "the aircraft is being repaired and will be inspected and certified before returning to service." McMahon left separately as well as a plane carrying talents like Hulk Hogan.

Lost in the controversy was the feel good moment WWE had been pushing for since the beginning of the relationship: Female wrestlers being able to perform in Saudi Arabia. While Natalya Neidhart had flown to the country for a June show with the international that they might wrestle, it did not come to pass. This time, Neidhart and Lacey Evans performed before the crown, albeit in more conservative gear than stateside (a long t-shirt with black tops that extended beyond the t-shirt to nearly the wrist). Both wrestlers seemed genuinely overcome by the magnitude of the moment.

Not everyone was pleased. Dana Ahmed of Amnesty International told *Newsweek* about concerns the organization had about the match: "WWE's first-ever women's match taking place in Riyadh is a prime example how the Saudi Arabian authorities are using elite sports to try to 'sportswash' their dire human rights record and image internationally."

As Trump's tenure as President rolled on, what was old was new again. Rallies, generally unheard of for a sitting President outside of election periods, and insults to rivals continued. Michael Bloomberg, a billionaire New York businessman and former three-time Mayor of New York City, flirted with a candidacy and ultimately joined for a short unsuccessful run. Having been in the same circles, Bloomberg's decision to run especially irked Trump, if his Twitter feed could be believed. He had a new nickname for Bloomberg, although somewhat uninspired: Mini, at 5'8." Bernie Sanders got off relatively light by Trump standards, he was just "crazy."

When NBC's Tom Brokaw cancelled his planned commencement speech at Sacred Heart University under sexual assault allegations in 2018, Linda McMahon stepped in. While many members of Trump's cabinet cycled in and out at his whim, one transition from the public sector gained more importance to his continued presidential hopes: Linda McMahon.

McMahon resigned from her role as Administrator for the SBA on April 15, 2019. There have been many departures from Trump's team since becoming President and many have left, or been forced to leave, in an unpleasant manner. McMahon's departure was a very pleasant experience for the viewer; from his Palm Beach home, Trump announced her departure. He said her work had been outstanding and that she'd be very helpful in the next year and a half towards re-election, while not yet announcing her next steps. She served without much controversy. Although speculated on immediately, McMahon was named Chairman of America First Action, a pro-Trump Super PAC, a key fundraising arm to support Trump's 2020 re-election bid.

Much of Trump's presidency had been under the specter of a potential impeachment. When an impeachment inquiry was finally announced as going ahead by Speaker of the House Nancy Pelosi, Linda McMahon was happy to crow about what a win it was for Trump's fundraising efforts on FOX Business: "When Nancy Pelosi announced that we were moving forward with the impeachment inquiry, in the next seven days, we raised seven million dollars." In case anyone's math was lacking, she explained that it was nearly a million dollars a day. She continued "That speaks, I think, volumes to how people are rallying around the President."

President Trump's February 2020 State of the Union Address was memorable for its theatrics and professional wrestling comparisons were not far behind. He awarded a "surprise" medal of honor to Rush Limbaugh, with Melania bestowing the medal on his neck, and an army wife was in the spotlight when, her husband returned from Afghanistan and greeted her in the balcony. *The Atlantic* described the evening as "emotional and vulgar."

Trump also had rivals to contend with: Tim Ryan of Ohio, who had been tweeting that he'd had enough and it was all fake, like professional wrestling, with Bill Pascrell of New Jersey, walked out, and Nancy Pelosi ripped up a copy of his speech while Trump basked in the applause.

By March 2020, historic impeachment proceedings seemed like an undercard to a bleak future. The world was ravaged in battling the Coronavirus and the wrestling industry was not exempt to the peripheral storyline.

While nearly all professional sports leagues and live event experiences went into a long hiatus, the wrestling business rolled on. With WrestleMania just a few weeks away, there was an uncertainty on if the show would be held. It was in WWE's training venue, the Performance Center, in Orange County, FL. Without any fans. This venue and city would be key to WWE remaining in compliance with its television contracts, which were to deliver live programming forty-nine out fifty-two weeks a year. While no other organization could imagine meeting this requirement in a world under lockdown or shelter in place orders, the Mayor of Orange County, Demmings deemed it as an essential business: "Originally, they were not deemed an essential business. With some conversation with the governor's office regarding the governor's order, they were deemed an essential business."

The State of Florida Office of Emergency Management put out a memo that the state has deemed "employees at a professional sports and media production with a national audience—including . . . athletes, entertainers, production team, executive team, media team" and others as essential. The order had come from Governor DeSantis. He said any conspiracy theories were unfounded and would like to see a variety of sports and media return to the state, such as a Nascar race and a televised golf game.

While there may not have been a conspiracy, many were quick to connect the dots, including Stephanie Coueignoux, an Emmy award-winning investigative journalist for Orlando's My News 13:

April 1: Governor DeSantis issues executive order for essential services after speaking with (President Trump)

April 9: Governor amended order to include professional sports and media production- including entertainers with a national audience.

Linda McMahon announces her Super PAC will spend

$18.5 million in Tampa and Orlando.

April 10: Reports come out Vince McMahon has decided to resume live TV in Orlando

Prior to the order, Vince McMahon provided flyers to talent to distribute to authorities that the company was providing essential media. The Sheriff was called to the facility multiple times and were informed that they had to shut down as they were not in compliance with the stay-at-home order. Upon request from *Fightful*, the Orange County Sheriff's department provided the following statement: "There are no reports written from that address by OCSO deputies in March or April, but we know that our deputies responded to that location several times in the last few weeks. Each time, they advised the business that they were not in compliance with the Executive Order and advised them that they would have to close down. On April 13, someone called to say there would be a taping at the location that evening. But by that time, an April 9 memo from the Florida Division of Emergency Management had already deemed those types of businesses "essential."

On April 9, America First Action PA, chaired by Linda McMahon, announced an investment of $26.2 million in battleground states. The planned spending in Florida and North Carolina would span from Labor Day to Election Day. Florida's $18.5 million portion of the spend would be split between the Tampa ($7.2 million) and Orlando ($11.3 million) markets. In noting a previous spend in the same release, Joe Biden was referred to as "sleepy." The next week's press release touted the launch of a campaign called "Beijing Biden" with an accompanying hashtag of #BeijingBiden.

Paul White, The Big Show, a long time WWE performer, best known for his massive height and storylines that have switched his stature from face to heel many times, was quick to support the company while promoting his forthcoming Netflix sitcom: "We feel an incredible responsibility, especially during times of hardship like this, to give our fans a way to escape . . . we say we're putting smiles on people's faces—yeah, that's become like a slogan, but that's in our job, our mandate, for the twenty-plus years that I've been at WWE. You always want to make sure that the crowd has the best show possible." The show must go on. On April 1, WWE partnered with the Ad Council on a public service announcement to raise awareness during the pandemic. The slogan: "Staying home saves lives."

Trump had to have been pleased with McMahon's efforts to keep things moving. In fact, he represented WWE in a conference call with Trump in early April, along with the commissioners or representatives of thirteen major sports leagues including the Ultimate Fighting Championship, Major League Baseball, the National Hockey League and the NFL. Details of the call were not disclosed but it was reported that Trump thinks sports is an important part of getting back to normal and he wants sports like the NFL to start on time or to resume to normal as soon as possible.

Word came that one league would not return: the XFL. The McMahon run league cited challenges in light of COVID-19 with returning after its shortened first season. The company filed for Chapter 11. The air was completely let out of the ball for the league informally deemed "MAGA Football."

In a whirlwind week, Trump named an advisory committee to reopen the country. It included many prominent commissioners of major sports leagues and also past rival, Mark Cuban. Two members of the committee were named as "Great" by Trump, Vince McMahon and the UFC's Dana White. The Middletown Press reported that Vince McMahon's wealth increased during the initial 3-months of the Coronavirus (March 18— June 17 2020) by 9.8 percent, or $177 million dollars.

Things began to unravel for WWE tapings in Florida: While good news came that networks would not require live shows every week and the company could tape shows on multiple days, it was reported that potentially twenty-four or more employees and performers had been infected with Coronavirus. The company continued to emphasize its importance in providing entertainment to fans, after the health of its staff of course.

As Joe Biden emerged as the democratic candidate, the value of every potential voter became important to the Trump campaign, even those potentially long ostracized. In appealing to evangelicals of color, those of Mexican heritage may be impossible to reach. However, one pastor quoted by the *Washington Post* thought that was not the case. Pablo Jimenez, the associate dean of a program for Hispanic ministry at Gordon-Conwell, noted Trump's WWE past, which is popular among Mexican Americans. "A lot of things he says, we find offensive. But it's a technique from pro wrestling . . . They know he's just playing 'the heel,'" Jimenez said. "The heel is the one who insults, who calls people names and who trolls people . . . You know these things, and you don't take it seriously. You know that he's just playing a role."

There was one more potential rival possibly on the horizon, Jesse Ventura. Although unlikely to make a statistically significant difference, it did bring things full circle for Trump. Ventura announced on Twitter on April

27, 2020 that he was considering a run for the White House in 2020 with the Green Party: "OK, I've decided I'm going to test the waters. IF I were going to run for president, the GREEN party would be my first choice. I've endorsed the party and I'm testing the waters."

In the midst of history, Black Lives Matter protests and civil unrest not seen in the United States for over fifty years (let alone the continued spread of the Coronavirus in much of the country), Donald Trump touted his employment numbers in June 2020. Linda McMahon tweeted that the numbers were great and that "We will continue to see the Great American comeback!"

When considering the unpredictable road of politics, pro wrestling, the McMahons and the Trumps, it's a McMahon that perhaps provides the best opportunity for reflection. Stephanie McMahon said in an August 2019 interview with *Fortune*: "It's a privilege and a responsibility to reflect society at large. WWE is ultimately a reflection of the world and we need to be representative of all cultures, all people."

One could say that politics is also a reflection of the world around us. What society puts in front of the mirror, both good and bad, and thus reflects back at us, is something we must consider in the 2020 Presidential Election season and beyond. And one thing is nearly certain, the aftershocks of a period that began in the late 1980s will continue to be felt into the unforeseen future.

BIBLIOGRAPHY

Cox News Services. Dems court young voters with celebs. July 27, 2004.

Krasselt, Kaitlyn. *The Middletown Press.* "Report shows CT billionaires increase wealth amid pandemic." June 29, 2020.

Jackman, Phil. *The Evening Sun.* "Rocky Balboa is tough, but he'll skip Andre the Giant, thank you." November 8, 1988.

Seemet, Patricia. *Hartford Courant.* "Fest gives fans a chance to go to the mat." October 31, 1994 .

Jacklin, Michele. *Hartford Courant.* "Credibility has pinned Weicker again." November 28, 1999.

Graham. David. *The Atlantic.* "The State of the Union as Spectacle." February 4, 2020.

Bump, Philip. *The Washington Post.* "Trump's NASCAR event was targeted at his base—but maybe he should have gone to a hockey game." February 18, 2020.

Ahmed, Tufayel. *Newsweek.* "WWE, Saudi Arabia 'Sportswashing' Country's 'Dire Human Rights Record' With First-ever Women's Match." October 31, 2019.

Otero-Amad, Farah. NBCNews.com "WWE hosts Saudi Arabia's first women's wrestling match." October 31, 2019.

Tindera, Michela. "At least 20 billionaires behind 'Dark Money' group that opposed Obama." October 26, 2019.

Riley-Smith, Ben. WWE blames 'mechanical issues' for delayed takeoff of plane carrying stars from Saudi Arabia after claims of row. November 5, 2019.

Wood, Graeme. *The Atlantic*. "The Brutal Truth Behind Trump's Love Affair With Saudi Arabia. November 18, 2018."

American Oversight Twitter: @Weareoversight. June 17, 2020. 6:18pm.

Leonnig, Garol; Dawsey, J. *The Washington Post*. "Ivanka Trump used a personal email account to send hundreds of emails about government business last year." November 19, 2018.

Breuniger, Kevin. "WWE confirms Saudi wrestling event in Q3 earnings report despite searing backlash over Jamal Khashoggi's death." October 25, 2018.

Gannett News Services. Young voters aim to be heard. February 4, 2004.

Jurgensen, Dan. "Come Together: Maybe not what Lennon had in mind." November 2 2003.

Kalinowski, Robert. *Citizen's Voice*. "Campaign registers 75 new voters." July 19, 2004.

Kane, Tara. "Young adults are looking for a reason to vote." June 23, 2004.

The Los Angeles Times. "More and more groups are 'getting out the vote.'" October 18, 2000.

Marvez, Alex. *South Florida Sun Sentinel*. "Foley, Layfield square off . . . in a debate." September 24, 2004.

Neuman, Johanna. "Politicians make use of wrestlers' hold on youths." August 22, 2004.

Ovalle, David. "Wrestlers take UM by storm, battle it out during debate." September 30, 2004.

Pratt, Richard. *The Gazette*. "Wrestlers chase voters." October 23, 2004.

Quintanilla, Michael. *The Los Angeles Times*. "The Stampede is On." January 12th, 2001.

Rayasam, Renuka. *Cox News Services*. "Hip-hop stars and wrestlers headline effort to tap youth vote." September 29, 2003.

Saunders, Hollie. "Young people want help getting politically involved." February 17, 2004.

Soler, Eileen. "Speaking of Debates." October 17, 2004.

Tarrant, David. *The Dallas Morning News*. "Wrestlers use influence to get young adults to the polls." February 15, 2004.

The Central New Jersey Home News. "Wrestlers, hip-hop artists form 'tag-team' to boost youth voting." September 28, 2003.

The Montgomery Advertiser. "Wrestler, secretary of state to encourage voting." May 20, 2002.

Varsallone, Jim. "Spotlight on Wrestling: WWF campaign successful getting people registered to vote." September 2, 2000.

Weiser, Carl. *Gannett News Services*. "Summit to probe how to get young people to vote." February 16, 2004.

Wilber, Del Quentin. "WWF eyes votermania." October 28, 2000.

Zaragoza, Luis. "Wrestler urges students to flex voting muscle." June 6, 2007.

Altimari, Daniela. *Hartford Courant*. "Murphy Slams McMahon over Trump Donation." February 10, 2012.

Star Tribune. "Our Perspective: eX-FL. Ventura should focus on day job." May 15, 2001.

Baden, Patricia. *Star Tribune*. "Losing XFL job wouldn't hurt Ventura, observers say." March 16, 2001.

Akers, John. Associated Press. "Ventura gets low marks as analyst." February 6, 2001.

Smith, Dane. *Star Tribune*. "Ventura's XFL job gets approval from state commissioner." December 12th, 2000.

Whereatt, Robert. *Star Tribune*. "Moe asks Hatch for ethics check on Ventura's XFL job." November 21, 2000.

Whereatt, Robert. *Star Tribune*. "Ethics." November 29, 2000.

McAuliffe, Bill. *Star Tribune*. "XFL ad may have violated Ventura contract." December 21, 2000.

Lentz, Jacob. *Electing Jesse Ventura: A Third-Party Success Story*. Lynne Riener Publishers. 2002.

Royce, Graydon, et. al. *Star Tribune*. "Event features some unlikely fans and much support for Ventura." August 2rd, 1999.

Weiner, Jay, et. al. *Star Tribune*. "Ventura may do 'Xtreme' color." November 16, 2000.

Brady, John. *Bad Boy: The Life and Politics of Lee Atwater*. ddison Wesley Publishing Co. 1997.

Rose, Gary L. *No Holds Barred: The 2012 Connecticut Senate Race*. Academica Press. 2013.

St. Cloud Times. Ventura has a new venture. November 17, 2000.

Doyle, Pat. *Star Tribune*. Wrestling role divides generations. August 24, 1999.

Royce, Graydon. *Star Tribune*. Jesse's Night Out. August 23, 1999.

Smith, Dane. *Star Tribune*. "Ventura will rule the ring as 'guest referee.'" July 15, 1999.

Royce, Graydon. *Star Tribune*. WWF ringmaster wins with Ventura. July 18, 1999.

Smith, Dane. *Star Tribune*. Ventura's WWF stint called into question. August 19, 1999.

The Winona Daily News. "The Body' back in wrestling ring, but for what?" July 13th, 1999.

Whereatt, Robert. *Star Tribune*. "Governor to do pre-ring promo." August 6, 1999.

The Winona Daily News. "Gov. Ventura will referee WWF match." July 15, 1999.

St. Cloud Times. Ventura plans return to the ring. July 13th, 1999.

St. Cloud Times. Ventura defends return to wrestling. July 14, 1999.

The Winona Daily Rider. Legislators express disappointment in Ventura's return to wrestling ring. July 18, 1999.

Vigdor, Neil. *Hartford Courant*. McMahon replaces Brokaw as Commencement Speaker. April 28, 2018.

Radelot, Ana. *Hartford Courant*. McMahon plans to divest. February 3, 2017.

Keating, Christopher. *Hartford Courant*. WWE's McMahon Gets Senate Approval for Board. February 12th, 2009.

Altimari, Daniela & Blair, Russell. *Hartford Courant*. August 14, 2016.

Haar, Dan. Hartford Courant. WWE Seeks State Aid to Help It Add Jobs. October 19, 2012.

Los Angeles Times. 'McMahon may toss in Ventura's XFL towel." March 15, 2001.

Hartford Courant. "Capital Watch: WWE Accuses Journal Inquirer of Libel." June 5, 2012.

Altimari, Daniela. *Hartford Courant*. "McMahon releases 2010 tax return." July 21, 2012.

Lee, Marla & Gosselin, Kenneth. *Hartford Courant*. "Cash for Cashet." April 9, 2012.

Keating, Christopher. *Hartford Courant*. "6 Big GOP Names Back McMahon. September 30, 2011.

Lender, Jon. *Hartford Courant*. "McMahon Quits State Board of Education. April 2, 2010.

Lender, Jon. *Hartford Courant*. "McMahon's unusual logic." April 4, 2010.

Keating, Christopher. *Hartford Courant*. "Wooing fans." October 31, 2010.

Altimari, Daniela. *Hartford Courant*. "Wrestling in New Ring: Politics." December 20, 2009.

Altimari, Daniela. *Hartford Courant*. "2 GOP Senate Hopefuls Admit Not Voting." September 22, 2009.

Pazniokas, Mark. *Hartford Courant*. "WWE Executive is Rell's Pick." January 15, 2009.

Hartford Courant. "Why Wrestle With Board Choices?" January 23, 2009.

Wrestling Observer Newsletter. September 13th, 2010; November 8 2010. March 5, 2018, March 12th, 2018, March 26, 2018, April 24, 2018, April 30, 2018, May 8, 2018, May 13, 2018, August

27, 2018, September 3, 2018, October 15, 2018. October 22, 2018, October 29, 2018, November 5, 2018, November 12, 2018, November 19, 2018, March 18, 2019, April 29, 2019, May 6, 2019, June 7, 2019, June 10, 2019, June 17, 2019, October 28, 2019, November 4, 2019, November 11, 2019, March 9, 2020

Pazniokas, Mark. *Hartford Courant*. "Key Rell Lobbyist Wrestles with Unusual Challenge." February 6, 2009.

Hartford Courant. "Congress." February 21, 2017

Altimari, Daniela. *Hartford Courant*. "Trump Putting State Into Play." August 12th, 2016.

Hartford Courant. "McMahon." December 8, 2016.

Altimari, Daniela. *Hartford Courant*. September 26, 2012.

Hartford Courant. " Our View: For Mr. Blumenthal, a tough road to senate." November 3, 2010.

Altimari, Daniella and Christopher Keating. *Hartford Courant*. "GOP Ally Stumps for McMahon." October 23, 2012.

Altimari, Daniela. *Hartford Courant*. "Trump." January 24, 2016.

Haigh, Susan. Associated Press. "GOP's McMahon ad targets Connecticut Obama voters." October 23, 2012.

Budoff, Carrie. *Hartford Courant*. "Campaign ads play to an audience. "September 20, 2000.

Collins, Gail. *Rocky Mountain Telegram*. "How well do you remember the year that was?" January 2, 2017.

Coulter, Ann. *Republican Herald*. "This is a job for Palin. June 13, 2010.

Sioux City Journal. "Trump chooses former WWE exec McMahon for SBA cabinet post." December 8, 2016.

The Spokesman Review. "Trump appointee to aid in re-election." March 30, 2019.

Blair, Russell. *Hartford Courant*. " McMahon." March 30, 2019.

Associated Press. "Christie campaigns in Conn. for Senate hopeful." October 23, 2012

Furst, Randy. *Star Tribune*. "Jesse ready for one last big ride?" September 13, 2015.

Marvez, Alex. *Scripps-Howard News Service*. "Wrestler-turned-politician-dangers." October 31, 2010.

Star Tribune."Ventura." October 8, 1999.

Brunt, Cliff. Associated Press. "Imagine Trump without the hair . . . it could happen." March 30, 2007.

Robinson, Eugene. *Asbury Park Press*. "Is the GOP now its own worst enemy? Kooky candidates could hand dem undeserved wins." August 15, 2010.

Budoff, Carrie. *Hartford Courant*. "GOP Challenger Confident Grappling In The Political Ring." November 2, 2000.

Jordan, Bob. *Asbury Park Press*. "Christie." November 7, 2010.

Standard-Speaker. "Romney isn't feeling republican love." September 24, 2012.

Jordan, Bob. *The Daily Journal*."Christie's Big Backers." August 1, 2015.

Lloyd, Jack. *Tallahassee Democrat*. "Slammy's the Grammy of pro wrestling." December 17, 1987.

Associated Press. "McMahon wrestles with wife's candidacy." August 7, 2010.

Freking, Kevin. Associated Press. "SBA nominee cites WWE experience." January 25, 2017.

Brubaker, Harold. *The Morning Call*. "It's Trump Plaza's turn to Cash Out." September 16, 2014.

Star Tribune. Trump Wins. "The Dismay. The Triumph." November 10, 2016.

Jacklin, Michele. *Hartford Courant*. Imagine Rep. Backlund? It's Too Hard. October 18, 2000.

The Boston Globe. WWE's Linda McMahon aims for smackdown of Dodd. September 17, 2009.

Linskey, Annie. *The Boston Globe*. Political gifts give investor among nation's top 20. June 5, 2015.

Arizona Republic. Sign me up as liking Trump's Shtick. April 21, 2011.

The Daily Item. Harrelson talks about his 'brutal' dinner with Donald Trump. October 30, 2017.

DePledge, Derrick. *Cincinnati Enquirer*. "Avoid a Smack-Down—Get out and Vote." August 31, 2000.

Davey, Monica, et. al. *The New York Times*. "Dennis Hastert sentenced to 15 months, and apologizes for sex abuse." April 27, 2016

Emmert Dose. *The Journal Times*. "As I See It." August 28, 2015.

Fry, Darrell. *Tampa Bay Times*. "Now it's Jesse 'The Governing Body' Ventura." November 8, 1990.

Egan, Mark. *The Ottawa Citizen*. "Republicans take aim at Trump bid." April 23, 2011.

Varsallone, Jim. *The Miami Herald*. "WWF campaign successful getting people registered to vote." September 2, 2000.

Colins, Gail. *The Journal News*. "From the Left: Voters aren't happy with Connecticut smackdown." October 29, 2012.

Journal and Courier. "Trump's GOP: Glitz, opulence and power. February 14, 2011.

McCartney, Anthony. *The Tampa Tribune*. "Political strategist favored the underdog." November 11, 2006.

Amata, A.J. Nino. *The Capital Times*. "Two wild cards that could throw the race to Donald Trump." August 17, 2016.

Balir, Russell. *Hartford Courant*. "Former Foes, McMahon, Murphy

Meet." January 13th, 2017.

Ventura, Jesse. *I Ain't Got Time to Bleed*. 2000. Signet.

Moore, Martha T. *Honolulu Star Advertiser*. "Ticket-splitters targeted in Conn." October 25, 2012.

Fournier, Ron, *Indiana Gazette*. "Buchanan plans to take fragile coalition with him." November 2, 1998.

Mathis, Deborah. News Press. "Americans hunger for truth." October 12th, 1999.

PBS News Hour. "Before 2016, Donald Trump had a history of toying with a presidential run." July 20, 2016.

Knight, Jim. *Philadelphia Daily News*. "Here, There & Everywhere." August 29, 1986.

Nelson, Bobo. *Detroit Free Press*. "Time is right for WrestleMania VI." March 30, 1990.

Bilotti, Carmine. *The Herald News*. "WWF on pay-per-view." March 24, 1988.

Herald & Review. "Quotable." June 20, 1994.

Honolulu Star Advertiser. "Our View: The 5 Worst Political Ads." November 2, 2012.

The Sunday Register. Atlantic City. March 27, 1988.

Los Angeles Times. Trump: Melding Politics and Entertainment.

December 6, 1999.

Lin, Jennifer. *The Republic*. "Trump: Power and money incarnate." December 13th, 1987.

The Philadelphia Inquirer. "Going to the mat." March 11th, 1988.

Ramos, Dante. *The Boston Globe Sunday*. "Character Sketch: Linda McMahon." August 15, 2010.

Butterfield, Fox. *Palm Beach Post*. "Trump developing broader dreams?" October 6, 1987.

Cohen, Nancy L. Delirium. *The Politics of Sex in America*. 2012.

Coulter, Ann. "Never trust a liberal over 3—especially a Republican." 2013.

Kazin, Michael. *Tampa Bay Times*. "Populism has moved from its roots." November 27, 1998.

Flint, Joe. *Los Angeles Times*. "WWE Chief Quits, Eyes US Senate." September 17, 2009.

Deangelis, Mary Beth. *The Charlotte Observer*. "'Nature Boy' may follow 'The Body.'" January 18, 2000.

The Miami Herald. "Jesse Ventura for President?" August 4, 2003.

Carlson, Margaret. *Pittsburgh Post Gazette*. "Round 1 for the wrestling queen." August 12th, 2010.

Burton, Cynthia. *The Philadelphia Inquirer*. "WrestleMania in a Conn.

race, with a Pa. tie." May 2, 2010.

Wilson, Mike. *The Miami Herald*. "The Man who would be Kingmaker." September 25, 1987.

Horrigan, Kevin. *St. Louis Post Dispatch*. "Politics in 'Jeopardy.'" April 27, 2008.

Contreras, Russel. *Wisconsin State Journal*. "Immigration a tool to attract fans in the US." April 1, 2012.

Lyons, Gene. *Santa Maria Times*. "Trump, swaggering supervillain of the GOP." August 10, 2015.

Bixenspan, David. Deadspin. "FBI Records Show Vince McMahon's Dad Caught on Tape Bragging About Threatening a Wrestle." March 27, 2017.

Kellman, Laurie. *Tallahassee Democrat*. "'The Donald' and 'The Body' dance around 'the question.'" January 8, 2000.

Dowd, Maureen. *Victoria Advocate*. Trump l'oeil tease. September 22, 1999.

The Herald News. "The King' Who Would be Memphis Mayor." April 8, 1999.

Lowry, Rich. *King Features*. "Our Donald Trump Moment." April 16, 2011.

Red Deer Advocate. "'Raw' tosses 'Impact' outta the ring. March 18, 2010.

TrumpMania

https://twitter.com/GovJVentura/status/1254783039642595330

https://twitter.com/i/status/1253146869028597761

Rocky Mountain Telegram. "'Nature Boy' meets with 'The Body.'" February 17, 2000.

West, Paul. *The Baltimore Sun*. October 8, 1999.

The Journal News. "Atwater." March 30, 1991.

South Florida Sun Sentinel. "Ventura has eye on White House." April 16, 2004.

Carlson, Doug. *The Tampa Tribune*. "Tossing Em Into the Ring." August 9 1992.

Schram, Martin. *The Newark Advocate*. "Pro wrestling comes to politics." August 19, 1992.

Cannon, Carl. *The Miami Herald*. "Is Bush's manager behind tawdry race?" November 6, 1988.

The Post Star, letters column. November 14, 1998.

Wolf, Alissa. *Boardwalk Beat*. November 13th, 1988.

Central New Jersey Home News. "And We Quote." November 8, 1998.

Fitzpatrick, Jackie. *San Francisco Examiner*. "The Lady and the Champs" June 6, 1993.

Taskin, Richard. *The Berkshire Eagle*. "Wrestling with cultural politics." April 27, 1988.

Nold Jr., James. *The Courier Journal.* "WrestleMania IV promises rage and revenge." March 25, 1988.

Snyder, Rod, *The Morning Call.* "Pro wrestling wants state deregulation." June 12, 1987.

The Philadelphia Inquirer. "Steel Wheels tour rolls to its finale." December 18, 1989.

Central New Jersey Homes News. "Weekend Attractions." October 28, 1988.

Associated Press. *The Body Politic.* "Ex-Wrestler Ventura grapples for mayor's office." November 5, 1990.

Toolen, Tom. *The Record.* "Wrestling has powerful hold on its audience." April 8, 1986.

Lloyd, Jack. *The Philadelphia Inquirer.* "The news from ringside. March 24, 1989."

Brooks, David. *Honolulu Star Advertiser.* "Trump learned his moves from professional wrestling." April 23, 2020.

Allen, Jessica. *The Wit and Wisdom of Jesse the Body/Mind Ventura.* Quill/William Morrow. 1999.

Darrow, Chuck. *Courier-Post.* "By George, it's trash-culture's new rage." October 30, 1988.

Bilotti, Carmine. *The Herald-News.* "Hogan meets The Giant today in WrestleMania III."

Associated Press. "Jeb Bush remarks expose immigration problem." April 11th, 2014.

Shea, Jim. *Hartford Courant*. "Our Lives (And Local TV) After Linda." October 28, 2012.

McEnroe, Colin. *Hartford Courant*. "McMahon." May 17, 2015.

Wolf, Alissa. *Asbury Park Press*. "Boardwalk Beat." October 23, 1988.

Altimari, Daniela. *Hartford Courant*. "McMahon Still in the GOP Storyline." July 22, 2013.

McMahon, Linda. *Hartford Courant*. "Focus on Enabling Growth, Small Business." January 26, 2013.

Lloyd, Jack. *The Philadelphia Inquirer*. "The return of 'Wrestlemania.'" April 4, 1986.

Spatz, David. *The Central New Jersey Home News*. "Trump Plaza Hotel hosts 'Superbowl of Wrestling.'" January 29, 1988.

Decker, Jonathan. *Great Dads: A Celebration of Fairness*. Adams Media Corporation. 2000.

Hartford Courant. Backlund getting ready to rumble. February 5, 1999.

Hartford Courant. "Wrestler." November 18, 2009

Kenosha News. August 15, 2000.

Meinert, Kendra. *Green Bay Press-Gazette*. The Donald brings flair- and hair- to Titletown. "June 25, 2009.

Dave Bryant's People & Places. *Fort Worth Star-Telegram*. February 5, 1991.

Bloom, David. *El Paso Times*. "Hulk Hogan to run for President in 2000." November 9, 1998.

Stewart, D.L. Dayton. *Daily News*. "Razzlemania." April 2, 1988.

McCollum, Charlie. *Knight Rider Services*. "It's fake, but hottest thing going." November 15, 1998.

Raasch, Chuck. *Daily Record*. "Today's politics: A shoot-out with no crowd." September 19, 1999.

Chadwick, Bruce. *Daily News*. "Hulk Hogan Fights Again. The World Wrestling Federation is on its way to Casino City." March 20, 1988.

Lupica, Mike. *Daily News*. Voters will wrestle with bad choices. November 1, 2010.

Wilkinson, David. Associated Press. "Whitman buries special tax on TV professional wrestling." March 18, 1997.

Darrow, Chuck. Courier-Post. "A.C.'s Wrestling Won't Mat-erialize." January 25, 1990.

McMahon, Linda. *Courier Post*. "Commentary: Lessons lead girls from locker room to boardroom." November 7, 2015.

Asbury Park Press. "WrestleMania." Sunday April 7, 2019.

Arizona Republic. "Top 2014 individual donors." January 11, 2015.

Wilkinson, Bud. Arizona Republic. Pro wrestling keeps its fans in a headlock. May 31, 1985.

Miga, Andrew. Associated Press. "Wrestling Exec Eyes Senate Race." Sept. 27, 2009.

"America First Action PAC Announces $26.2M Investment in Battleground States." April 9, 2020.

Bethel, B.J. *Sydney Morning Herald*. "Trump honed his skills as a carnival spruiker in pro wrestling's ring." January 28, 2018.

Commonwealth of Pennsylvania State Government Ad Hoc Committee of the House of Representatives June 11, 1987 (Transcript)

WWE *Ruthless Aggression* Documentary. 2020.

Gail-Kim Irvine @gailkimITSME Twitter 12/12/2019 https://twitter.com/gailkimITSME/status/1205226077523718146

Haring, Bruce. *Deadline*. "President Donald Trump Holds Phone Call With Sports Czars As Rumors Swirl Over Seasons Ending And Possibly Cancelled." April 4, 2020.

Lambert, Jeremy. *Fightful*. WWE Told Multiples Times By Orange County Sheriff To Close Down Before "Essential Business Order. April 14, 2020.

Nolasco, Stephanie. Fox News. "The Big Show says WWE, deemed 'essential' has a responsibility during 'times of hardship.'"

April 14, 2020

Roberts, Daniel. Yahoo! Finance. "NFL team owner Shad Khan still supports Trump on economy, not on social issues." October 10, 2019.

Stabile, Angelica, FOX Business. "Pro-Trump super PAC raises nearly $1M a day after impeachment inquiry announcement. October 31, 2019.

WhatCulture. "12 things we learned from Jim Ross' *Under the Black Hat.*"

Zauzmer, Julie; Boorstein, Michelle. *The Washington Post*. "The Trump campaign wants to win the votes of evangelicals of color." April 13, 2020.

Orange County Government Updates COVID-19 update April 13, 2020 (Facebook).

WrestleMania IV Press Conference. WWE Network.

https://twitter.com/davidbix/status/1249875084560515072

https://twitter.com/NewsGuyGreg/status/1250540257684193280

https://mobile.twitter.com/StephanieCNews/status/1250135431691341824

Bernstein, Andrea. *American Oligarchs: The Kushners, the Trumps, and the Marriage of Money and Power.* W.W. Norton & Co. 2020

McLeod, Saul. *SimplePsychology. Type A Personality*. 2008; updated 2014.

Nark, Jason. Phily.com. "When Trump made boxing—and Atlantic City—great again." 5/27/17 Schwartz, David.

Casino Connection AC. "Plaza Suite: History of Trump Plaza." 2/2/2010.

Shoemaker, David. *The Ringer*. "The Story of Vince McMahon As told by Vince McMahon." 6/2/2016 WWE.com Donald Trump Superstar Stats.

Argus-Leader. Sports Talk. Feb. 25, 1988.

Associated Press. 'Macho Man' lives up to billing in WrestleMania IV. March 8, 1988.

Associated Press. "Leonard Camacho fight back on for March 1." December 5, 1996

Darrow, Chuck. *Courier-Post*. "'The Last American Hero' goes to the mat again." March 25, 1988.

DeVito, B, Layton, J. *WWF WrestleMania: The Official Insider's Story*. 3/6/2001.

Eskenazi, Gerald. *New York Times*. "The Morning Call: Pay-per-view TV next blockbuster?" March 4, 1988.

The Courier-News. "NBA Notebook." March 27, 1988.

Gustkey, Earl. "Leonard-Lalonde Bout Never Captured Public." November 19, 1988.

Kent, Bill. *The Philadelphia Inquirer*. "Going to the mat." March 11, 1988.

Lloyd, Jack. *The Philadelphia Inquirer*. "A WrestleMania run." March 25, 1988.

Osnos, Peter. *The New Yorker*. "Personal History: Editing Donald Trump." November 3, 2019.

Quinn, Liam. *Daily Mail*. "Film from 1988 WrestleMania shows Donald Trump beside the alleged mobster he claims not to know." November 2, 2016.

The Daily Times. "Drama Builds for WrestleMania IV." March 13, 1988. WrestleMania IV Event Program

Beck, Ken. *The Tennessean*. Pro wrestling gets class. 1/19/1992.

DeVito, B, Layton, J. WWF WrestleMania: The Official Insider's Story. 3/6/2001.

Donlon, Brian. *Gannett News Services*. 'WrestleMania V' is cable's biggest. April 2, 1989.

Grossman, Hillary. *Florida Today*. "Wrestling for Ratings." March 30, 1989.

Hanley, Robert. "Copter Crash Kills 3 Aides of Trump." 10/11/1989.

Interview with Dawn Maestas, Godiva. 7/24/17

Kerr, Peter. *New York Times*. "Now It Can Be Told: Those Pro

Wrestlers are Just Having Fun." 2/10/1989.

Mascitti, Al. *The News Journal*. "Brother, can you spare a mil?" March 27, 1991.

Lambert, Jeremy. Fightful. *Donald Trump names 'The Great' Vince McMahon, Dana White, More as Advisors to Restart Economy.* April 14, 2020

McGough, Peter. *Muscular Development*. "The WBF Story- Why the IFB's Greatest Ever Challenge Failed." 4/3/2014

Muchnick, Irv. *Wrestling Babylon: Piledriving Tales of Drugs, Sex, Death, and Scandal.* 11/16/2010.

NYPost.com. "A complete collection of the best Donald Trump New York Post covers." 2/16/1990

O'Malley & Collin Inc. *Chicago Tribune*. "That's entertainment." March 6, 1991.

O'Sullivan, Dan. *Vice Sports*. "The Forgotten Steroid Trial That Almost Brought Down Vince McMahon." 7/10/2015

Sandomir, Richard. *The New York Times*. "TV SPORTS; A Legendary Flop for Clashers." (3/3/1992).

Segal, David. "What Donald Trump's Plaza Deal Reveals About His White House Bid." 1/16/2016

Shales, Tom. *Green Bay Press-Gazette*. Hype grapples with megabucks. April 6, 1989.

The Morning Call. Timeline: Jimmy 'Superfly' Snuka and the death of Nancy Argentino. 1/3/2017. The Pro-Wrestling Chronicle. HISTORY: THE DEFINITIVE HISTORY OF THE WBF. (12/27/2005).

The Pro-Wrestling Chronicle. "History: The Definitive History of the WBF." 12/27/2005

Venezia, Joyce. Associated Press. "21,000 WrestleManiacs flock to Atlantic City. April 3, 1989."

Whitehouse, Beth. *Asbury Park Press*. "WrestleMania V. Fans wonder: Did Hulk tame the savage breast?" April 3, 1989.

Wilson, J., Johnson, W. *Chokehold: Pro Wrestling's Real Mayhem Outside the Ring*. Xlibris; First Edition, September 2, 2003.

WrestleMania V Event Program

Wrestling Observer Newsletter issues 5/10/1989; 6/24/1991; 7/22/1991; 12/23/1991; 8/25/1997

WrestlingData.com

WrestlingFigs.com

WarriorLynx

http://forum.wrestlingfigs.com/thread/338975/

Zidan, Karim. "Sports on Earth. Trump's MMA Tactics Sound Familiar." 8/6/2015

TrumpMania

Wrestling Observer Newsletter, 4/4/1988

WrestlingData.com[Text Wrapping Break]

Television/ Pay-per-view programs/ Media

Lapsed Fan Podcast.

30 Week Journey to WrestleMania: WrestleMania IV.

Something to Wrestle With Bruce Prichard. Episode 23: The Million Dollar Man

Syndicated WWF Programming: WrestleMania IV Report. February 1988.

WWF Prime Time Wrestling. USA Network. Airdate: 3/21/1988.

ABOUT THE AUTHOR

Lavie Margolin has followed professional wrestling since 1988. His writing in the industry includes pieces for WrestlingInc, the Wrestling Observer, PW Ponderings and through his own website, lioncubjobsearch.com.

In his other life, Lavie possess a master's degree in Adult Learning and teaches a career development course at a university in New York.

Printed in Great Britain
by Amazon